The New York Times

IN THE HEADLINES

Gun Rights

FINDING THE BALANCE

THE NEW YORK TIMES EDITORIAL STAFF

Published in 2021 by New York Times Educational Publishing
in association with The Rosen Publishing Group, Inc.
29 East 21st Street, New York, NY 10010

First Edition

The New York Times
Caroline Que: Editorial Director, Book Development
Cecilia Bohan: Photo Rights/Permissions Editor
Heidi Giovine: Administrative Manager

Rosen Publishing
Megan Kellerman: Managing Editor
Xina M. Uhl: Editor
Brian Garvey: Art Director

Cataloging-in-Publication Data
Names: New York Times Company.
Title: Gun rights: finding the balance / edited by the New York Times editorial staff.
Description: New York : New York Times Educational Publishing, 2021. | Series: In the headlines | Includes glossary and index.
Identifiers: ISBN 9781642824124 (library bound) | ISBN 9781642824117 (pbk.) | ISBN 9781642824131 (ebook)
Subjects: LCSH: United States. Constitution. 2nd Amendment—Juvenile literature. | Firearms—Law and legislation—United States—History—Juvenile literature. | Gun control—United States—History—Juvenile literature. | Firearms ownership—United States—Juvenile literature. | Firearms owners—Legal status laws, etc.—United States—Juvenile literature.
Classification: LCC KF3941.G86 2021 | DDC 323.4'3—dc23

Manufactured in the United States of America

On the cover: An attendee examines various guns at a booth during the National Rifle Association convention in Dallas, May 4, 2018; Tamir Kalifa/The New York Times.

Contents

Introduction

THE BILL OF RIGHTS — the first ten amendments of the Constitution — was ratified in 1791. The Second Amendment reads: "A well regulated Militia, being necessary to the security of a free State, the right of the people to keep and bear Arms, shall not be infringed."

The interpretation of the Second Amendment and the application of gun rights has been hotly contested. By looking at the perspectives of those on opposite sides of the debate, readers can come to a better understanding of this complex issue.

In 2008, the Supreme Court took on a case in which the District of Columbia had banned the possession of handguns in the home. The District of Columbia had also required that any lawful firearms in the home had to be disassembled or fitted with a trigger lock in order to make them impossible to use. The court's decision, in District of Columbia v. Heller, clarified the meaning of the Second Amendment. It stated that the amendment protects an individual's right to own a firearm regardless of service in a militia. This right must be for lawful purposes such as self-defense within a person's home. But this decision did not end the controversy or the court cases surrounding the Second Amendment.

The divisive issue of gun rights has ardent defenders on both sides: the side that demands regulation or complete removal of firearms and the side that fights against any such restriction of gun ownership. The devastating toll of gun-related deaths includes thousands of suicides and thousands of murders each year as well as a smaller number of accidental deaths. The deadliest shootings can involve large numbers of people, such as the killing of twenty children and six adults at Sandy Hook Elementary School in Newtown, Conn.,

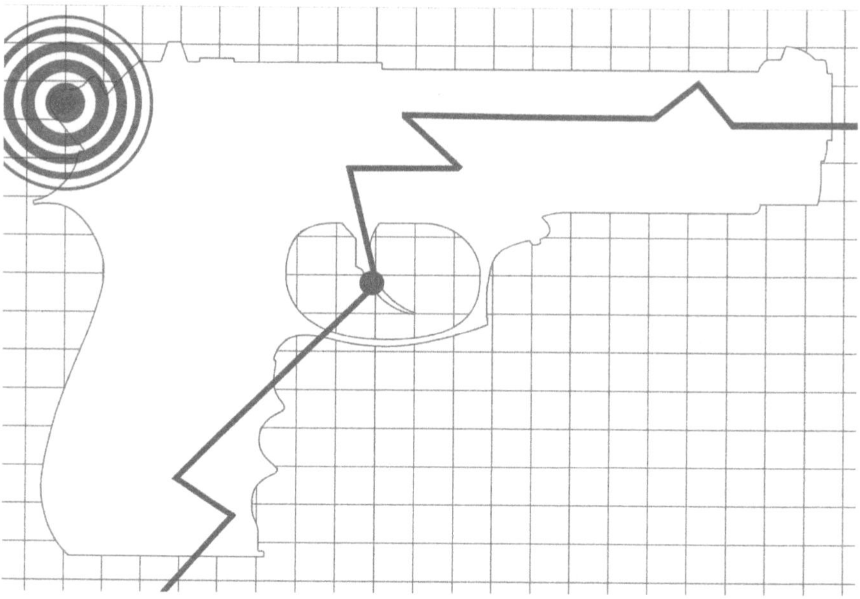

ELENA SCOTTI

in 2012. Whether mass shootings happen in schools, theaters, businesses or elsewhere, every time one occurs there is a renewed outcry for increased legislation to prevent such murders in the future. The National Rifle Association, or N.R.A., is the most strident voice against any such legislation.

The articles collected here look at the issue of gun rights from different viewpoints and explore a number of related issues. Chapter 1 examines gun laws from the federal and state perspectives. This includes decisions by individual states, the Supreme Court and discussions by lawmakers. The gun industry itself, including gun manufacturers and marketplaces such as individual shops and gun shows, also figure into this discussion.

Chapter 2 focuses on the terrible toll of gun violence, including the school shootings in Newtown, Conn., and Parkland, Fla. There's also an examination on the individual level by a father whose son was killed by a shooter at his college. This man's account delves into the complexities of advocating for gun control, gun ownership and how one's stance on gun rights can change with more education on the issue.

Chapter 3 looks at numerous factors that affect the rights of gun owners, such as felony convictions and mental health issues. For those who seek to have their gun rights restored, the road back to legal firearm ownership can be challenging depending on the state. As reporter Michael Luo writes, "all of these laws are complicated and often obscure." This issue is further complicated because, Luo adds, "law enforcement agencies generally do not systematically track these restorations." Without supporting data, the debate on when to limit, restore or deny gun rights to those seeking restoration is that much more difficult.

Chapter 4 examines the latest legislative efforts for gun control and provides fact checks and debates on the issue. The Democratic candidates for the 2020 presidential election appear to be in agreement on pursuing a more aggressive gun control position. Meanwhile, private businesses are seeking to restrict open-carry in their stores. And with a new Democratic majority in the Virginia General Assembly, gun rights activists continue to make their voices heard: In January 2020, more than 20,000 people rallied at the Virginia Capitol to protest gun control proposals. Whether or not the state Democratic majority will have a significant impact on gun rights remains to be seen.

CHAPTER 1

Federal and State Gun Laws

State and federal governments have been dealing with gun rights issues for decades. The debate rages between those who support unfettered access to guns and those who want to strictly regulate them. Even the issue of background checks for gun buyers is hotly contested. The N.R.A. fears that such restrictions, designed to keep felons and the mentally ill from gun ownership, is a slippery slope that may end in increasingly restrictive gun control.

An Ominous Reversal on Gun Rights

EDITORIAL | BY THE NEW YORK TIMES | MAY 14, 2002

USING A FOOTNOTE in a set of Supreme Court briefs, Attorney General John Ashcroft announced a radical shift last week in six decades of government policy toward the rights of Americans to own guns. Burying the change in fine print cannot disguise the ominous implications for law enforcement or Mr. Ashcroft's betrayal of his public duty.

The footnote declares that, contrary to longstanding and bipartisan interpretation of the Second Amendment, the Constitution "broadly protects the rights of individuals" to own firearms. This view and the accompanying legal standard Mr. Ashcroft has suggested — equating gun ownership with core free speech rights — could make it extremely difficult for the government to regulate firearms, as it has done for decades.

That position comports with Mr. Ashcroft's long-held personal opinion, which he expressed a year ago in a letter to his close allies at the National Rifle Association. But it is a position at odds with both history and the Constitution's text. As the Supreme Court correctly concluded in a 1939 decision that remains the key legal precedent on the subject, the Second Amendment protects only those rights that have "some reasonable relationship to the preservation of efficiency of a well-regulated militia." By not viewing the amendment as a basic, individual right, this decision left room for broad gun ownership regulation. The footnote is also at odds with Mr. Ashcroft's pledge at his confirmation hearing that his personal ideology would not drive Justice Department legal policies.

It is hard to take seriously Mr. Ashcroft's assertion that the Bush administration remains committed to the vigorous defense and enforcement of all federal gun laws. Mr. Ashcroft, after all, is an official whose devotion to the gun lobby extends to granting its request to immediately destroy records of gun purchases amassed in the process of conducting Brady law background checks even though they might be useful for tracking weapons purchases by suspected terrorists.

The immediate effect of the Bush Justice Department's expansive reading of the Second Amendment is to undermine law enforcement by calling into question valuable state and federal gun restrictions on the books, and by handing dangerous criminals a potent new weapon for challenging their convictions. What it all adds up to is a gift to pro-gun extremists, and a shabby deal for everyone else.

Tennessee Expands Gun Rights

BY KATHARINE Q. SEELYE | JUNE 15, 2009

CITIES AND COUNTIES across Tennessee are preparing this week to deal with the fallout from a raft of pro-gun bills recently signed into law in the state, where Republicans are flexing their new-found strength in the legislature.

Among the new laws is one that would allow people who have gun permits to carry guns in all public parks in the state. Another would exempt from federal regulation guns and ammunition made in Tennessee and kept within its borders.

The measure with the most immediate impact may be the guns-in-parks law. Cities and towns have the chance to opt out of it by Sept. 1 and are beginning debate now about whether to do so. The City of Nashville is scheduled to start hearings on Tuesday.

The measure allowing guns in state parks went into effect Friday and will probably go into effect in national parks starting in February. It applies to the 220,000 Tennesseans who hold gun permits as well as visitors from other states with valid permits.

The law exempting Tennessee from federal gun regulations, while having little immediate effect, may have broader implications down the road. It comes as part of a states'-rights movement that tries to test the limits of federal power. The Tennessee bill is nearly identical to one signed into law in Montana and similar to ones under consideration in other states. Since Montana's law does not take effect until Oct. 1, the one in Tennessee, which takes effect July 1, could become the first test case in the courts.

"The purpose of this bill is to let people know we have state sovereignty and the federal government has no business telling us what to do," State Senator Mae Beavers, a Mount Juliet Republican who sponsored the bill, said in an interview.

The new laws in Tennessee, coming soon after the recent shooting in a church in Kansas of a doctor who performed late-term abortions, and the shooting of a guard at the Holocaust museum in Washington, have prompted intense comment on local Web sites like www.commercialappeal.com, www.knoxnews.com and www.tennessean.com.

Brian Malte, director of state legislation for the Brady Campaign to Prevent Gun Violence, said Tennessee already had among the least restrictive gun laws in the country. Still, Mr. Malte said, the flurry of pro-gun bills was highly unusual and reflected a push by the gun lobby in a state with a newly sympathetic legislature, of which both houses are now controlled by Republicans.

Gun-rights advocates say expanded rights are needed so that law-abiding citizens can protect themselves in more situations. The new Tennessee laws also include measures that will allow permit holders to carry guns in bars and restaurants, if they are not drinking alcohol, and to carry a loaded rifle or shotgun in their vehicles if the ammunition is in the magazine but not in the chamber, although it can be in the chamber for purposes of self-defense.

The new law exempting the state from federal gun regulations is less about the Second Amendment, involving the bearing of arms, than the 10th Amendment, reflecting a states'-rights movement that is picking up steam across the country.

"The short-term practical effect will be nil," Kevin R.C. Gutzman, who teaches history at Western Connecticut State University and supports the states'-rights movement, said of Tennessee's federal-exemption bill. "But in the long term, or medium term, it's having the effect of provoking a conversation about the allocation of powers between the federal and state governments."

The measure, called the Tennessee Firearms Freedom Act, says that firearms and ammunition made and sold within the state, and stamped "Made in Tennessee," are beyond the jurisdiction of the federal government. The theory is that if firearms are not sold across state lines they cannot be considered part of interstate commerce and are therefore exempt from federal regulations.

Those regulations cover things like documentation on the sale and shipment of firearms. They also bar possession by certain people, like felons and the mentally ill. Gun owners would still be subject to state laws.

Gov. Phil Bredesen, a Democrat, who vetoed the guns-in-bars bill but was overridden, said in a statement late Friday that he would allow the exemption bill to become law without his signature. The bill "represents a fringe constitutional theory" that will be thrown out of court, Mr. Bredesen said, but letting it become law may speed that challenge and yield clarity sooner. He said that in the meantime, the federal Bureau of Alcohol, Tobacco, Firearms and Explosives would enforce federal regulations, and he predicted confusion for gun makers, dealers and importers.

Gun-control advocates say these efforts to exempt states from federal gun laws will have a limited effect because few federal laws exist anyway. Those that do exist, said Daniel Vice, senior lawyer at the Brady Center to Prevent Gun Violence, involve background checks and what he called "basic record-keeping." But evading any federal laws, Mr. Vice added, could make it easier for criminals to get guns.

Whatever the practical result of Tennessee's new gun laws, they may well serve a political purpose: firing up the conservative base before next year's state, local and Congressional elections.

"The Republicans are trying to embarrass the Democrats," said John G. Geer, a political scientist at Vanderbilt University in Nashville.

"They want to put these proposals on the table not only because they believe in guns, but they want to force the Democrats to come out as anti-gun," Professor Geer said. "You can see the attack ads forming already. The Republicans have won this issue."

Supreme Court Still Divided on Guns

BY ADAM LIPTAK | MARCH 2, 2010

WASHINGTON — At least five justices appeared poised to expand the scope of the Second Amendment's protection of the right to bear arms on Tuesday, judging from comments at an unusually intense Supreme Court argument.

By its conclusion, it seemed plain that the court would extend a 2008 decision that first identified an individual right to own guns to strike down Chicago's gun control law, widely considered the most restrictive in the nation.

While such a ruling would represent an enormous symbolic victory for supporters of gun rights, its short-term practical impact would almost certainly be limited. Just how much strength the Second Amendment has in places that regulate but do not ban guns outright will be worked out in additional cases.

The new case, McDonald v. Chicago, No. 08-1521, was a sequel to the 2008 decision in District of Columbia v. Heller, which placed limits on what the federal government may do to regulate guns. The issue before the court in the new case was whether the Second Amendment also applied to state and local laws. It appeared that at least the justices in the Heller majority would say yes without reservation because they considered the rights protected in the Second Amendment as basic as those in other provisions of the Bill of Rights.

"If it's not fundamental, then Heller is wrong," said Justice Anthony M. Kennedy, who was in the majority in Heller.

Justice John Paul Stevens, who wrote a dissent in Heller, suggested Tuesday that important questions remain unresolved.

"I'm asking you what is the scope of the right to own a gun?" he said. "Is it just the right to have it at home, or is the right to parade around the streets with guns?"

Heller itself struck down parts of the gun control law in the District of Columbia, then the strictest in the nation. But the majority opinion, by Justice Antonin Scalia, suggested that all sorts of restrictions on gun ownership might pass Second Amendment muster.

Justice Stephen G. Breyer, who also wrote a dissent in Heller, peppered the lawyers with questions about how the court might apply the Second Amendment to the states in a limited way. The Second Amendment says, "A well regulated militia, being necessary to the security of a free state, the right of the people to keep and bear arms, shall not be infringed."

Drawing on the first clause of the amendment, Justice Breyer said that a right tied to state militias might be worthy of protection, while the right to bear arms "to shoot burglars" might not be.

The lead plaintiff in the case, Otis McDonald, has said he wants to keep a handgun in his home for protection from drug gangs. Justice Breyer asked Alan Gura, a lawyer for residents of Chicago challenging its gun control law, whether the city should remain free to ban guns if it could show that hundreds of lives would be saved. Mr. Gura said no.

Justice Scalia objected to the inquiry. A constitutional right, he said, cannot be overcome because it may have negative consequences.

But Justice Scalia was less receptive to an idea that has excited constitutional scholars in recent months. "What you argue," he told Mr. Gura, "is the darling of the professoriate, for sure, but it's also contrary to 140 years of our jurisprudence."

Justice Scalia was referring to Mr. Gura's assertion that the court has been making parts of the Bill of Rights applicable to the states in the wrong way.

The Second Amendment, like the rest of the Bill of Rights, originally restricted only the power of the federal government. The Supreme Court later ruled that most but not all of the protections of the Bill of Rights applied to the states under the due process clause of the 14th Amendment, one of the post-Civil War amendments.

Many judges and scholars, including Justice Scalia, have never found that methodology intellectually satisfactory. "Due process," after all, would seem to protect only procedures and not substance. The very name given to the methodology — substantive due process — sounds like an oxymoron.

Mr. Gura, supported by scholars all along the political spectrum, argued that the court should instead rely on the 14th Amendment's "privileges or immunities" clause, which says that "no state shall make or enforce any law which shall abridge the privileges or immunities of citizens of the United States." There is evidence that the authors of the clause specifically wanted it to apply to allow freed slaves to have guns to defend themselves.

Justice Scalia was unimpressed. He said Mr. Gura should focus on winning his case rather than remaking constitutional law.

"Why do you want to undertake that burden," Justice Scalia asked, "instead of just arguing substantive due process, which as much as I think it's wrong, even I have acquiesced in it?"

Unless, the justice added, Mr. Gura was "bucking for a place on some law school faculty."

James A. Feldman, a lawyer for the City of Chicago, urged the justices to treat the Second Amendment differently from its cousins because it concerns a lethal product. "Firearms, unlike anything else that is the subject of a provision of the Bill of Rights, are designed to injure and kill," Mr. Feldman said.

Now it was the chief justice's turn to give advice to the lawyer before him.

"All the arguments you make against" applying the Second Amendment to the states, Chief Justice John G. Roberts Jr. said, "it seems to me are arguments you should make in favor of regulation under the Second Amendment. We haven't said anything about what the content of the Second Amendment is beyond what was said in Heller."

States' Rights vs. Gun Rights

ROOM FOR DEBATE | BY THE NEW YORK TIMES | MARCH 2, 2010

In Room for Debate, The Times invites knowledgeable outside contributors to discuss news events and other timely issues.

THE SUPREME COURT heard oral arguments on a major gun control case on Tuesday. The issue in the case, McDonald v. City of Chicago, is whether the Second Amendment protects the individual right to keep and bear arms against state and city gun laws. The case is considered a sequel to a Supreme Court decision in 2008, District of Columbia v. Heller, which limited what the federal government can do in restricting gun rights.

Will a decision against Chicago, which has banned handguns since 1982, make it far more difficult for states and cities to impose gun-control measures (even measures less stringent that an outright ban)? Are there implications that go beyond gun rights?

Eugene Volokh, law professor, U.C.L.A.

James Alan Fox, criminology professor, Northeastern University

AN END TO GUN BANS

Eugene Volokh is a professor of law at the University of California, Los Angeles. He is the founder and co-author of The Volokh Conspiracy blog. Three of his articles on the right to keep and bear arms were cited by the majority opinion in District of Columbia v. Heller.

Of the 50 states, 44 have state constitutional provisions that expressly secure a right to keep and bear arms. At least 40 of them clearly protect an individual right, aimed partly at self-defense.

Yet state courts interpreting those provisions have upheld the great majority of all modest gun controls that they have considered. They have struck down some total gun bans, and some other restrictions that dramatically affect people's abilities to defend themselves. But less stringent restrictions have almost always been upheld.

Likewise, federal courts applying D.C. v. Heller have upheld the great majority of the restrictions that they have considered, including all of the less stringent ones.

Thus, for instance, courts have upheld bans on particular kinds of semi-automatic firearms (so-called "assault weapons") precisely because the bans left people free to own many different kinds of other handguns, rifles and shotguns that were just as effective for self-defense.

The same seems likely to happen with federal review of state and local gun bans, if the U.S. Supreme Court concludes that the Second Amendment — like the First Amendment, the Fourth Amendment and most of the rest of the Bill of Rights — applies to the states via the Fourteenth Amendment.

Total handgun bans would be struck down. The same might happen to some of the most restrictive gun controls, such as laws banning gun possession by non-citizens (even ones who legally live in the U.S.). But less stringent gun controls, whether or not wise as a matter of policy, are almost certain to be upheld.

WHAT CHICAGO ACHIEVED

James Alan Fox is the Lipman Family Professor of Criminology, Law and Public Policy at Northeastern University and joined in an amicus brief in McDonald v. Chicago.

In statistical data analysis as in everyday experience, first impressions can be deceiving. A superficial glance at the Chicago murder rate in the years following implementation of its handgun ban indicates that homicide counts increased sharply through the late 1980s and into the early 1990s — a fact noted by those challenging the efficacy (as well as constitutionality) of the ban.

The premature conclusion was that law-abiding Chicagoans were being deprived of their right and ability to protect themselves from armed criminals, who easily obtained guns through illegal channels.

However, a closer examination of the crime trends shows that the surge in homicides largely involved criminals targeted by other criminals, reflecting the crack-related gang wars that had exploded in

Chicago as in cities across America. By contrast, homicides occurring in residential settings declined, especially those involving family members as perpetrators.

While Chicago residents, particularly those living in high crime neighborhoods, might feel the need to protect themselves with guns, the fact is, guns purchased and kept in the bedside drawer for defensive purposes are all too often used instead to settle a domestic dispute. The Chicago handgun ban directly addresses this peril of private handgun ownership.

In preparing an amicus brief in support of the handgun ban, I analyzed detailed homicide data for Chicago and dozens of other American cities, adjusted not only for population size but also for each municipality's demographic and socio-economic profile.

My analysis of the Chicago data found that, compared with other cities, the handgun ban had lowered the rate of gun homicide. In fact, over the past 25 years, there were an estimated 800 to 1,000 fewer murders in Chicago because of the handgun ban.

Whatever the outcome of the ongoing legal challenge, the public debate over whether gun ownership increases or decreases the risk of violence may never be settled. In the meantime, let's hope Chicago will be permitted to maintain its ban on handgun ownership, saving dozens of lives annually for many years to come.

Out of State Guns

OPINION | BY ANDREW ROSENTHAL | APRIL 9, 2012

LAST WEEK, YET another school shooting served as a reminder of how desperately America needs to have a conversation about guns — though naturally we won't have one due to the lobbying efforts of the National Rifle Association.

This week's reminder comes from New York, where a 33-year-old man shot four police officers early Sunday. He fired his 9-millimeter Browning semiautomatic handgun 12 times and the police said they found a military-style assault rifle and a defaced 22-caliber revolver in the man's apartment.

All four officers are expected to recover. But Mayor Michael Bloomberg pointed out: "We have now had eight — that's correct, eight — members of the department shot in the last four months and this is the second time in the last 24 hours police have been fired upon by armed assailants."

He added: "All the shootings have a disgraceful fact in common: all were committed with illegal guns that came from out of state. And that is the case with nearly every shooting in our city."

Those who oppose restrictions on gun ownership might argue that New York's strict laws don't seem to stop this sort of crime. Others, including me, see it as a national problem when someone can buy a firearm in a state that's soft on guns, carry it into another state and shoot four cops. It's a national problem that requires national standards.

Congress, of course, has been headed in exactly the other direction. Last November, the House passed a bill that, as Gail Collins put it in a column, requires "states with strict gun regulations to honor concealed-weapon carry permits issued in states where the gun rules are slightly more lax than the restrictions on who can dispense ice cream cones from a truck."

It's a race to the bottom. New York would have to allow someone with a Florida concealed-carry permit to tote a hidden gun around Times Square.

Law-enforcement agencies across the country oppose the bill, in part because shoddy record-keeping would make it difficult for cops to verify that someone actually has an official permit from another state. But only 154 members of the House voted against it.

It seems likely this bill will die in the Senate, but that's not enough. Congress needs to stop catering to the N.R.A. and establish sensible across-the-board criteria for licensing.

ANDREW ROSENTHAL is the Editorial Page editor of The Times, overseeing the newspaper's Opinion section.

State Focus and Infusion of Funding Buoy Gun Control Advocates

BY ERIC LICHTBLAU | JAN. 3, 2016

ALEXANDRIA, VA. — With President Obama poised to act on his own authority to try to stem gun violence, his gun control allies are using big-money donors and shifting tactics to try to remake the political landscape in the national gun debate, challenging and sometimes even besting the powerful National Rifle Association in state-by-state battles.

The newfound momentum reflects a strategy to steer clear of a Republican-led Congress that has proved unwilling to touch existing federal gun laws after years of intense lobbying on both sides of the debate.

With tens of millions of dollars to spend thanks to backers like Michael R. Bloomberg, the former mayor of New York, gun control groups have secured a number of surprising recent successes in Connecticut, Delaware and elsewhere. And they are now looking to state and local officials to win approval for tougher background checks and other measures from Nevada to Maine.

The N.R.A. remains the dominant force in much of the country, spending more than $32.5 million last year on campaigns and lobbying. It has shown continued muscle in stopping new restrictions and loosening existing ones in many localities. But the political landscape has become more hotly contested as a result of the gun control groups' shift in focus and infusion of cash, operatives on both sides say. The axiom that gun control is a losing political issue does not always hold true anymore.

"The money was almost exclusively on the pro-gun side of the fence before, and we were always accused of spending our way to victory," said Richard Feldman, a former N.R.A. executive who leads the Independent Firearms Owners Association. "Now the other side has these

DREW ANGERER FOR THE NEW YORK TIMES

Ladd Everitt leading gun violence prevention activists in a protest this month outside the headquarters of the National Rifle Association in Fairfax, Va.

resources from Michael Bloomberg to get involved in these state and local races, something they didn't have before."

The organization Everytown for Gun Safety — which received $36 million in contributions last year, with the biggest chunk coming from Mr. Bloomberg — has eclipsed a number of older gun control groups in publicity and influence. In its latest push, the group is funding an ad campaign for players from the National Basketball Association to speak out against gun violence.

The group, created in 2014 after the slaughter in 2012 of 26 children and adults at an elementary school in Newtown, Conn., says its supporters have now grown to three million nationwide, including survivors of shootings, mayors, police officers, celebrities and rank-and-file supporters. It has chapters in all 50 states, with registered lobbyists in 31 of them, adopting a structure used to great effectiveness by the N.R.A. itself. Mr. Bloomberg has pledged to spend at least

$50 million of his own money in the group's push for tougher gun restrictions — a level of spending that Jennifer Baker, an N.R.A. official, called "obscene."

In some races, gun control advocates are outspending the deep-pocketed N.R.A. And after the mass shooting in San Bernardino, Calif., and earlier rampages at a Planned Parenthood facility in Colorado, a community college in Oregon and a church in Charleston, S.C., gun control advocates said they planned to expand their push for stiffer local restrictions still further. They believe their cause was buoyed last month when the Supreme Court let stand an ordinance in a Chicago suburb that bans semiautomatic assault weapons.

Mr. Obama is expected to move ahead as soon as this week with a series of executive actions modifying federal gun laws. On Tuesday, gun control activists are expected to gather at the White House to discuss possible action, and on Thursday — a day before the fifth anniversary of the shooting of former Representative Gabrielle Giffords in Arizona — he will participate in a town-hall-style meeting on gun violence that will be shown on CNN. But the measures he is considering would be a modest tweaking of the law compared with the more sweeping changes that gun control groups are pushing for at the state and local levels.

The growing importance of state gun laws was made clear last month when Gov. Dannel P. Malloy of Connecticut announced that he would act on his own to bar anyone on the government's terrorism watch lists from buying a gun. Congress refused to take that step nationwide.

Mr. Malloy, a Democrat, said in a telephone interview that afterward, other governors looking to follow his lead on the issue had contacted him.

Changing gun policies "is easier to do on a state-by-state basis than it is on a national level, because Congress is gerrymandered to such an extent," Mr. Malloy said.

Gun control supporters gained another big win in Virginia last month when the state's attorney general, Mark R. Herring, a Democrat, barred anyone who holds a concealed-handgun permit in 25 other states from using it to carry a firearm in Virginia.

Virginia, despite its reputation as a pro-gun state, also produced a victory for gun control supporters last month when Jeremy McPike, a Democrat from suburban Washington and a political novice running on a gun control platform, was elected to the State Senate. Mr. McPike's campaign was helped by $1.5 million from Everytown. The group blanketed the area with ads promoting Mr. McPike's record on gun control, and he was elected despite an F grade from the N.R.A.

"It takes muscle to counteract the muscle of the N.R.A.," he said in an interview.

Mr. McPike grew up in a family of hunters, and as a volunteer firefighter he said many of his colleagues were vocal gun-rights advocates. But his views have been shaped by his own history: He said he remembered responding to an emergency call for a teenager who had accidentally shot himself in the groin, and he said his brother had committed suicide at the age of 16 with a family gun.

"At some point, you can't sit on the sidelines anymore," he said. "You've got to find a way to effect change."

In the closing weeks of his race and two other campaigns in Virginia that hinged on guns, the N.R.A. and gun control groups all sent people to the local districts to rally voters. Candidates backed by the N.R.A. won both of the other races, helping Republicans hold a majority in the State Senate. The N.R.A. saw the results as a rebuke of Mr. Bloomberg's organization.

"They got their butts kicked in Virginia," Ms. Baker said. "You spend all that money, and all you have to show for it is one win? That's complete and utter failure."

Gun control advocates have not given up on Washington completely. They have met repeatedly with White House officials to urge Mr. Obama to issue an executive order to tighten some gun measures, and the president will meet with Attorney General Loretta E. Lynch and the F.B.I. director, James B. Comey, on Monday to discuss his options. He is limited in what he can do, however, and the advocates see their best chance for change at the state level — particularly in pushing ballot initiatives that put gun control questions to voters.

The shift away from Washington is rooted in Congress's rejection in 2013 of expanded background checks that were proposed in the wake of the shootings in Newtown.

Mr. Obama said the failure to pass gun control legislation after the Connecticut tragedy was one of the biggest disappointments of his presidency, and gun control advocates said the jolt from that rejection made them realize that changes were all but impossible in Congress.

After that defeat, "we took a step back, and we realized we had to go state by state," said John Feinblatt, the president of the Everytown group.

Everytown's big footprint, however, worries even some fellow gun control advocates. They say some local officials in Massachusetts, Rhode Island and elsewhere have resented the perception of a high-profile, billionaire liberal like Mr. Bloomberg trying to change their gun laws.

"I see them as a lightning rod," said an official with another gun control group, speaking on the condition of anonymity because of concerns about alienating supporters. "They're stirring up this opposition, and the N.R.A. as a result is putting more resources into its state strategy."

Mr. Feinblatt said Everytown was changing the nature of the debate. He likened the focus on the states to the push for same-sex marriage, which began with a small number of states approving it before the Supreme Court struck down the Defense of Marriage Act in 2013 and it spread more quickly.

The strategy carries risks. The N.R.A. has five million members and boasts of a political base that is willing to turn out at the polls for a single issue: gun control.

With policies varying from one jurisdiction to the next, each side has a scorecard of victories to show why it believes it is winning the debate.

The N.R.A. points to 95 bills passed last year nationwide that it considers favorable to gun enthusiasts and hunters.

Mr. Bloomberg's group can point to laws passed in nine states last year to keep guns out of the hands of domestic abusers, the defeat of numerous bills that would have facilitated concealed-carry permits and, most critically, approval of a measure that expanded background checks in Oregon. It was the sixth state to pass a background check measure after the shootings in Newtown, and the 18th over all.

In Delaware, Gov. Jack Markell, a Democrat, signed a measure in October aimed at keeping guns out of the hands of domestic abusers; it was personally pushed by Ms. Giffords, who started a gun safety group after she was shot in the head in a mass shooting in 2011.

In Michigan, Gov. Rick Snyder, a Republican, vowed in November to veto — for a second time — a hotly debated bill that would allow permit-holders to carry concealed weapons in schools.

The next big battleground is Nevada, where a record number of signatures set up a vote this year on an initiative to impose a statewide background check. After that on the list of targets is Maine, where gun control advocates say they are confident they will soon have enough signatures to get a background check initiative on the state ballot.

N.R.A. officials say they are not worried.

"We'll see what happens," Ms. Baker said. "We know they're going to spend a lot of money, but I don't see any groundswell of support."

Supreme Court Will Review New York City Gun Law

BY ADAM LIPTAK | JAN. 22, 2019

WASHINGTON — The Supreme Court said on Tuesday that it would review a New York City gun law that limits residents from transporting their guns outside their homes, its first Second Amendment case in nearly a decade and a test of the court's approach to gun rights after the arrival of Justice Brett M. Kavanaugh in October.

Justice Kavanaugh, who replaced the more moderate Justice Anthony M. Kennedy and created a reliable five-member conservative majority, has an expansive view of gun rights. His presence most likely means that the Supreme Court will start exploring and perhaps expanding the scope of the Second Amendment.

"It could be a landmark case with major implications for gun policy," said Adam Winkler, the author of "Gunfight: The Battle Over the Right to Bear Arms in America." "The case could articulate broad principles about the Second Amendment, and especially the Second Amendment outside the home."

Court scholars said Justice Kavanaugh's replacement of Justice Kennedy could lead to an abrupt lurch from the court's previous decisions.

"This is just the first case but not likely the last case where at least four justices open the way to a major ruling that could limit gun safety laws," said Michael Waldman, the author of "The Second Amendment: A Biography," referring to a Supreme Court rule requiring four votes to add cases to its docket.

The New York City ordinance challenged in the new case allows residents with so-called premises licenses to take their guns to one of seven shooting ranges within the city limits. But the ordinance forbids them to take their guns anywhere else, including second homes and shooting ranges outside the city, even when they are unloaded and locked in a container separate from ammunition.

The Supreme Court's new majority seems ready to continue a project begun in 2008, when the court, by a 5-to-4 vote, established an individual right to keep guns in the home for self-defense. That decision, District of Columbia v. Heller, was both revolutionary and in its way quite limited. Exactly what the Second Amendment protects has been in dispute ever since.

Justice Antonin Scalia's majority opinion in the Heller decision included an important limiting passage that was almost certainly the price of Justice Kennedy's fifth vote. "Nothing in our opinion," Justice Scalia wrote, "should be taken to cast doubt on longstanding prohibitions on the possession of firearms by felons and the mentally ill, or laws forbidding the carrying of firearms in sensitive places such as schools and government buildings, or laws imposing conditions and qualifications on the commercial sale of arms."

Since the Heller decision, lower courts have overwhelmingly upheld state and local gun control laws. The Supreme Court, in turn, has refused to hear appeals from those decisions. Justice Kavanaugh's arrival changed that.

Last year, dissenting from the court's decision not to hear a Second Amendment case, Justice Clarence Thomas wrote that the court was abdicating its duty to protect an important constitutional right.

"As evidenced by our continued inaction in this area," he wrote, "the Second Amendment is a disfavored right in this court."

"The right to keep and bear arms is apparently this court's constitutional orphan," Justice Thomas wrote. "And the lower courts seem to have gotten the message."

Three city residents and the New York State Rifle and Pistol Association sued to challenge the law but lost in Federal District Court in Manhattan and in the United States Court of Appeals for the Second Circuit. A unanimous three-judge panel of the Second Circuit ruled that the ordinance passed constitutional muster under the Heller decision.

In urging the Supreme Court to hear their appeal in the case, New York State Rifle and Pistol Association v. City of New York, No. 18-280, the challengers said the restrictions imposed by the New York City ordinance were unique in the nation and made no sense.

"Only New York City flatly prohibits its residents from removing their lawfully purchased and duly registered handguns from the city limits, even to transport them (unloaded, and locked up) to second homes at which they are constitutionally entitled to possess them, or to out-of-city shooting ranges or competitions at which they are constitutionally entitled to hone their safe and effective use," the challengers' brief said.

"That prohibition does not even make sense on its own terms," the brief said. "It has the perverse consequences of forcing New Yorkers to leave their handguns behind in their vacant residences whenever they leave the city for an extended period of time."

Lawyers for the city responded that the law was justified by public safety considerations. Before 2001, their brief said, the city offered a license that allowed owners to take their guns to shooting ranges outside the city.

The Police Department, the brief said, "observed widespread abuses." Firing ranges in the city must keep detailed records, the brief said, but people with the old licenses who were found with guns outside their homes could claim to be headed to a range outside the city that did not keep such records.

Mayor Bill de Blasio, responding to a reporter's question about the Supreme Court's decision to hear the case, said at a news conference on Tuesday that the city would vigorously defend its law.

"We, every single day, are working to make this the safest big city in America," he said. "We need the laws that we have that protect against guns being on our streets and we will fight to protect ourselves, that's the bottom line."

Mr. Waldman said he was surprised the Supreme Court agreed to hear such a minor Second Amendment case when it has ducked some major ones.

"It's a city ordinance, not a state law," Mr. Waldman said. "This particular rule is unusual. It may be the only one of its kind in the country."

"The justices," he said, "may see this as a way to start addressing gun rights outside the home in a quirky and incremental manner."

The court will hear arguments in the case in its next term, which starts in October, and may not issue a decision until 2020. But Tuesday's decision to hear the case sent a message about a new era in the court led by Chief Justice John G. Roberts Jr.

"The Second Amendment is alive and well in the Roberts court," Mr. Winkler said.

WILLIAM NEUMAN contributed reporting from New York.

Defying N.R.A., Texas Lieutenant Governor Favors Background Checks on Private Gun Sales

BY NEIL VIGDOR
PUBLISHED SEPT. 6, 2019 | UPDATED SEPT. 7, 2019

Dan Patrick, a Republican, has promoted his A-plus grade from the National Rifle Association.

LT. GOV. DAN PATRICK of Texas publicly endorsed expanding the state's background checks to private gun sales on Friday, defying the National Rifle Association — a group that had previously given the conservative an A-plus grade for his Second Amendment bona fides.

Mr. Patrick, a Republican who was elected to a second term in 2018, went so far as to say during an interview on Friday with The Dallas Morning News that he was "willing to take an arrow" from the gun lobby.

Mr. Patrick's stance on expanding background checks followed a cycle of gun violence in the state, where gun culture is entrenched and transcends political affiliation.

It came less than a week after a gunman terrorized motorists near Odessa, Tex., killing seven people and wounding at least 21 more with an assault-style rifle that he obtained from a private seller in Lubbock, Tex., despite failing a background check in 2014 for a mental health issue. Earlier in August, 22 people were killed in a shooting rampage at a Walmart in El Paso in which a gunman targeted Hispanics.

"That gap of stranger to stranger we have to close, in my view," Mr. Patrick told The Morning News, speaking about gun sales. "When I talk to gun owners, N.R.A. members and voters, people don't understand why we allow strangers to sell guns to total strangers when they have no idea if the person they're selling the gun to could be a felon, could be someone who's getting a gun to go commit a crime or could be a potential mass shooter or someone who has serious mental issues."

Mr. Patrick's endorsement of expanded background checks came with a major caveat, according to The Morning News. Gun owners would not be required to conduct a background check when transferring a firearm to a family member, and friends would also be exempt — though the lieutenant governor acknowledged that could be abused.

Mr. Patrick's office did not immediately respond to a request from comment later Friday.

The N.R.A.'s Institute for Legislative Action panned Mr. Patrick's policy shift, which it said parroted the agenda of a prominent gun control group, Everytown for Gun Safety, which was started and financed by the former New York City mayor Michael R. Bloomberg.

"With due respect, Texas Lt. Gov. Dan Patrick's 'proposals' would resurrect the same broken, Bloomberg-funded failures that were attempted under the Obama administration," the N.R.A. said in a statement on Friday. "Like most political gambits, Lt. Gov. Patrick's 'solution' precedes his possession of the facts, including this critical concession by the Obama administration: Criminalizing private firearm transfers would require a massive, governmental gun registration scheme."

Gun control advocates said that closing the loophole on private gun sales was long overdue and represented a message to the Trump administration and Senator Mitch McConnell, the majority leader, about the need for sweeping reform at the national level.

"Look, the political ground is shifting," John Feinblatt, president of Everytown for Gun Safety, said in an interview Friday. "It's time for the Senate to get the memo. The truth is the N.R.A. has never been weaker. What you're seeing is elected officials, many of whom were closely aligned with the N.R.A., turning their back on the N.R.A. and choosing to be with the public rather than the gun lobby."

A number of top Republicans in Texas — from the governor, Greg Abbott, to Senator Ted Cruz and Mr. Patrick — faced significant criticism for their position and statements on guns following the Aug. 31 shooting rampage in Odessa.

Not long after the bloodshed in West Texas, a 2015 video resurfaced of Senator Cruz firing an assault-style rifle at an Iowa shooting range with bacon wrapped around the gun's hot barrel and then eating it. Mr. Cruz was a presidential candidate at the time.

"Of course in Texas, we cook bacon a little differently than most folks," Mr. Cruz said in the video, posted on a conservative website, adding, "Machine gun bacon."

In 2015, responding to a report in The Houston Chronicle, Mr. Abbott said on Twitter that he was "embarrassed" that Texas was second in the nation to California in new gun purchases. "Let's pick up the pace Texans," Mr. Abbott wrote on Twitter.

On Thursday, Mr. Abbott issued eight executive orders that he said would improve the state's red flag system for keeping guns out of the hands of dangerous criminals and better assess threats.

The measures require the Texas Department of Public Safety to develop standard intake questions for law enforcement officers to ask callers reporting suspicious activity and to train the police to assess threats.

The orders also tie future state grants received by counties to the timely reporting of criminal convictions to a state database. By 2020, 90 percent of convictions must be reported to the state within seven days, or a county would lose funding. By 2021, it must be done within five days.

But the executive orders signed by Mr. Abbott do not touch on gun laws, including background checks on private sales of firearms.

Mr. Abbott's office did not immediately respond to a request for comment about his stance on Mr. Patrick's suggestion that background checks be required for private sales.

Mr. Patrick told The Morning News, "Look, I'm a solid N.R.A. guy," but warned that Republicans could feel the wrath of voters in Texas and nationally on the issue of gun control. Five Republican members of Congress from Texas have already bowed out of running for re-election in 2020.

"Someone in the Republican Party has to take the lead on this," Mr. Patrick said.

The N.R.A. said in its statement that Mr. Patrick's proposal was misguided.

"Instead of trampling the freedom of law-abiding Americans, the government should focus upon actual solutions: fixing our broken mental health system, prosecuting known criminals and enforcing the existing gun laws that require follow-up whenever a prohibited person tries to buy a firearm," the N.R.A. said.

Lawmakers Court Trump on Gun Safety, With Some Appealing to His Ego

BY SHERYL GAY STOLBERG

PUBLISHED SEPT. 20, 2019 | UPDATED SEPT. 21, 2019

WASHINGTON — In a phone call with President Trump about gun safety legislation last week, Senator Joe Manchin III made an unusual offer: If Mr. Trump signed onto a background check bill that he and Senator Pat Toomey have been pushing for six years, the president could claim the naming rights for himself.

"This won't be Manchin-Toomey," Mr. Manchin recalled telling the president, referring to the measure that would expand background checks for gun buyers. "This is going to be the Common Sense Gun Bill of 2019 by President Trump."

With Mr. Trump expected to decide as early as next week whether he will defy the National Rifle Association and embrace a bill to expand background checks for gun purchases, Mr. Manchin, Democrat of West Virginia, is hardly the only lawmaker appealing to the image-conscious president. In meetings and phone calls with Mr. Trump and his advisers, backers of various gun safety bills have been waging a full-scale Washington courtship rooted in policy, politics and a little bit of presidential ego.

Speaker Nancy Pelosi and Senator Chuck Schumer, the top two Democrats in Congress, tried to tap into Mr. Trump's penchant for drama, promising to join the president for a "historic signing ceremony at the Rose Garden" if he abandoned his veto threat and got behind a more expansive, House-passed background checks bill.

Mr. Toomey, Republican of Pennsylvania, has appealed to "inherent logic," he said, making the case "on the merits" of using background checks to keep guns from criminals during a string of

ANNA MONEYMAKER/THE NEW YORK TIMES

Senators Joe Manchin III and Christopher S. Murphy, both Democrats, are long-time advocates of legislation expanding background checks.

conversations with the president, most recently at the White House Thursday.

And Senator Chris Murphy, Democrat of Connecticut and a central player in the background checks negotiations along with Mr. Manchin and Mr. Toomey, has told the president that with 90 percent of the public favoring expanded background checks, there would be "enormous benefit to him if he was willing to be the guy who brought this to completion."

When Mr. Manchin volunteered to take his name off the background checks bill, Mr. Murphy said, the three senators were huddled around a speakerphone, talking to Mr. Trump from Mr. Toomey's Capitol hideaway office.

"The president is a guy who thinks about branding," Mr. Toomey said. "I think we just want to make it clear to the president that if he was going to do this, that he should get credit for it."

Gun safety has long been one of the most intractable issues in Washington, but it catapulted to the forefront of the congressional agenda after a series of mass shootings over the summer. Democrats immediately demanded the Republican-controlled Senate pass a bill that had already moved through the House and would require all gun buyers to undergo background checks. But that bill remains stuck in the Senate, where Senator Mitch McConnell, the Republican leader, refuses to take it up, citing Mr. Trump's veto threat.

The somewhat narrower Manchin-Toomey bill would extend background checks to all commercial sales, including those at gun shows and over the internet. But that bill has fallen twice to a Senate filibuster, once in 2013 and once in 2015. Only two Republicans who have previously voted in favor of it — Mr. Toomey and Senator Susan Collins of Maine — remain in the Senate today.

Despite those obstacles, the political landscape around gun safety does appear to be changing. The N.R.A. is in a weakened state, mired in internal conflict and facing investigations into possible abuse of its tax-exempt status. The gun safety movement is ascendant, fueled by student activism in the wake of last year's mass shooting at Marjory Stoneman Douglas High School in Parkland, Fla.

And several newly elected Republicans, including Senators Mitt Romney of Utah and Mike Braun of Indiana, have called for expanded background checks in the wake of the summer shootings. Senator Lindsey Graham, Republican of South Carolina and a close ally of the president, is supporting a different type of gun safety legislation known as a "red flag" bill, and has warned Mr. Trump it was untenable to tell the public there was nothing he could do, "because the shootings are going to keep coming."

Ms. Collins, who said she has been in frequent contact with the president's advisers though not Mr. Trump himself, said he is convinced that "there are a lot of responsible, common sense gun safety provisions that could be bundled together that we could pass."

But both Republicans and Democrats agree that nothing will pass without Mr. Trump's support. The president is said to be reviewing a package of ideas presented to him by White House advisers. But he is keeping his views to himself, and his earlier public statements have been all over the map, in keeping with his history of flip-flops on the gun issue.

At first, after back-to-back massacres in El Paso and Dayton in early August, Mr. Trump said there was "tremendous" support for "really common-sense sensible, important background checks" and bragged that he could overcome the longstanding Washington gridlock on the issue.

"There's never been a president like President Trump," he said then.

"At that point, he was positively over the moon about background checks," said Mr. Murphy, who sponsors the Senate version of the House background checks bill.

But more recently, the president has walked back those enthusiastic comments, while critics of the Manchin-Toomey bill have raised two primary objections. They say the current system, which relies on federally-licensed firearms dealers conducting background checks, imposes a burden on rural buyers who live far from such dealers. And they warn that background check records could be used to create a national firearms registry, which they deeply oppose.

Earlier this week, William P. Barr, the attorney general, circulated a proposal on Capitol Hill designed to address those objections. The plan would create a new class of "licensed transfer agents" who would not sell guns, but would be authorized by the government to conduct background checks. And sellers, not firearms dealers or transfer agents, would retain the records, so they could not be used to create a registry.

In interviews, Senators Graham, Manchin, Toomey and Murphy all said Mr. Barr seemed serious, and that the plan formed the foundation of a potentially workable compromise.

"As long as it enables him to do his job and the Department of Justice to do it's job, I'm fine," Mr. Manchin said.

MADDIE MCGARVEY FOR THE NEW YORK TIMES

People protested against Mr. Trump's visit to Dayton, Ohio, after nine people were killed in a mass shooting.

"I've told him what Barr is working on seems to be sensible to me," Mr. Graham said, recounting his most recent conversation with the president on the issue. "I don't know exactly what the final product is. I will support whatever the president supports."

But the White House took pains to distance itself from Mr. Barr's proposal, and emphasized that it does not have Mr. Trump's blessing.

And any compromise in the Senate will be difficult to achieve. Mr. Toomey will have to bring in his colleagues from the right, who are leery of anything that smacks of gun control, and Mr. Murphy will have to bring in his colleagues from the left, who are demanding Senate passage of the stricter House bill and do not want to hand the president any political victories just as Mr. Trump is seeking re-election.

"I said, 'Mr. President, I'm as hard-line as you come on guns, and so my hope is that if I signed onto a compromise, that other people may be willing to take a hard look at this," Mr. Murphy said.

In the meantime, proponents are hoping to appeal to Mr. Trump's oft-stated desire for a big deal.

"My gut tells me that the president wants to do something meaningful to do more to keep guns out of the hands of people who should not have them," Mr. Toomey said.

Clashing Senate Reports and New Questions on the N.R.A.

BY DANNY HAKIM | SEPT. 27, 2019

A NEW 77-PAGE REPORT released Friday morning by Democrats on the Senate Finance Committee called the National Rifle Association "a foreign asset," said it had put its tax-exempt status at risk and undercut the gun group's efforts to distance itself from a controversial 2015 Moscow trip undertaken by some of its board members and supporters.

The findings, however, sharply split the committee along political lines — hardly a surprise, given the N.R.A.'s stalwart support for Republicans and growing anger among Democrats at the group's resistance to gun control measures.

In a 19-page rebuttal, Republicans on the committee, which is led by Senator Charles E. Grassley of Iowa, said the Democrats' report "attempts to paint a picture of the National Rifle Association with facts and innuendo that together actually demonstrate little to nothing."

The clashing assessments are the latest chapter in a year of turmoil for the N.R.A., which is facing investigations by Democratic attorneys general in New York and Washington, D.C., is mired in a bruising legal battle with its former ad firm, and has weathered a leadership battle and a stream of damaging leaks about its spending practices that have unnerved even some of its own donors and supporters.

William A. Brewer III, an outside counsel for the N.R.A., said the Democrats' report "promotes a politically motivated and contrived narrative," adding that "an avalanche of proof confirms that the N.R.A., as an organization, was never involved in the activities about which the Democrats write."

While the Democrats on the committee undertook the investigation, they conferred with Republicans, who reviewed most of the documents they obtained. The Democrats' report provided new detail on the extent to which the group was penetrated by Maria Butina, a Russian who pleaded guilty last year to taking part in a covert effort to infiltrate American conservative groups.

A top N.R.A. board member was even made aware ahead of the 2015 trip that Ms. Butina facilitated part of the visit by using her connections to Russia's Federal Security Service, or F.S.B., the main successor agency to the K.G.B. But documents provided to the committee by the N.R.A. suggested some at the highest levels had concerns about Ms. Butina. One N.R.A. official warned Donald Trump Jr., after a 2016 interaction with Ms. Butina: "I understand that someone introduced a Russian gal to you this week. I'll fill you in this week but I would steer clear if she tries to reach out to you."

While the official was not identified, two people with knowledge of the matter said it was Chris Cox, who was the N.R.A.'s top lobbyist and heir apparent until he departed earlier this year amid a leadership dispute with Wayne LaPierre, the N.R.A.'s longtime chief executive. Mr. Cox did not respond to requests for comment.

The N.R.A. has insisted that its leadership did not support the Moscow trip, which was ostensibly an effort to foster closer ties between gun-rights supporters. The N.R.A.'s delegation included both a former and a future N.R.A. president, and they visited two officials sanctioned by the American government at the time: Dmitry Rogozin, then a deputy prime minister, and Igor Shchyogolev, a special assistant to Vladimir Putin, the Russian president.

Senator Ron Wyden of Oregon, the ranking Democrat on the Finance Committee, said Friday that members of the delegation "may have violated U.S. sanctions," a notion Republicans refuted.

While the N.R.A.'s leadership has tried to distance itself from the 2015 trip, email traffic and a flurry of transactions reviewed by The New York Times earlier this week undercut claims that Mr. LaPierre and other leaders were not supportive. In the months after the trip, facing unpaid expenses of more than $21,000, N.R.A. officials had one prominent member of the delegation, Pete Brownell, write checks to pay costs related to the trip, but also transferred the same amount of money back to Mr. Brownell. The circuitous transactions later raised internal legal concerns among N.R.A. lawyers.

The series of transactions were overseen by a close aide to Mr. LaPierre, who said in a 2016 internal email obtained by The Times that they were approved by Mr. LaPierre. The N.R.A. said this week that the aide had misrepresented Mr. LaPierre's support.

The Democrats' new report cast further doubt on the N.R.A.'s efforts to disavow the trip, highlighting a letter from Allan Cors, then the N.R.A.'s president, on N.R.A. letterhead, in which he wrote that two of the trip's attendees "will represent the N.R.A. and its five million members." The letter was written to Alexander Torshin, a political patron of Ms. Butina.

Andrew Arulanandam, a spokesman for the N.R.A., said, "Certain N.R.A. members made the trip of their own accord. The record reflects it was not an official NRA trip."

Democrats on the committee said they would pursue a second investigation examining the N.R.A.'s broader spending practices, and also planned to refer some of the issues raised in the report to the Internal Revenue Service, which is seen as unlikely to take action.

"During the 2016 election, Russian nationals effectively used the promise of lucrative personal business opportunities to capture the N.R.A. and gain access to the American political system," Mr. Wyden said in a statement. "The totality of evidence uncovered during my investigation, as well as the mounting evidence of rampant self-dealing, indicate the N.R.A. may have violated tax laws."

But the Republican assessment, after opening with a broadside against the Obama administration and its Russia policies, cast aside such concerns.

"Following two and a half years of endless, feverish speculation about so-called collusion that cast suspicion on any and all things

Russian, the Minority report at issue attempts to paint a picture of the National Rifle Association with facts and innuendo that together actually demonstrate little to nothing," Republicans said.

New detail emerged in the report about the extent to which Ms. Butina and Mr. Torshin gained trust in the N.R.A., even as some officials like Mr. Cox appeared to have misgivings. In email traffic, Donna Keene, the wife of an N.R.A. board member and former president, referred to them as "dear friends" of the couple and said building ties to Russia was "N.R.A. business."

Pete Brownell, who was first vice president of the N.R.A. board when he attended the Moscow trip, learned ahead of time that Ms. Butina had ties to the F.S.B. Paul Erickson, a Republican operative and a boyfriend of Ms. Butina, told Mr. Brownell in an email that Ms. Butina had "moved heaven & earth" with the F.S.B. to secure Mr. Brownell a tour of an arms factory. Mr. Erickson said Ms. Butina was able to expedite the process "probably because most of the F.S.B. agents 'assigned' to her want to marry her."

Democrats also raised concerns about Mr. Brownell and other attendees pursuing personal business interests on what was ostensibly a good-will tour backed by the N.R.A., though Republicans said blending private and N.R.A. business on a trip was not inappropriate.

Ryan Repp, a spokesman for Mr. Brownell's company, the gun retailer Brownells, said in a statement that Mr. Brownell "sought out and obtained compliance guidance, including checking with the government, and followed that guidance before, during and after the trip."

"He went to support the N.R.A. as the incoming president, and would not have gone if it was not an N.R.A. trip," he added. "Pete received absolutely no business for his company as a result of this trip. He has fully cooperated with all inquiries."

The Republican report said, "It is fair to analyze the wisdom of traveling to Russia in December 2015 to meet with high ranking officials," but added that issues raised in the Democrats' analysis were minor at worst.

Mr. Wyden disagreed.

"This was an official trip undertaken so N.R.A. insiders could get rich — a clear violation of the principle that tax-exempt resources should not be used for personal benefit," he said. "The I.R.S. needs to examine these findings."

In a Face-off With the N.R.A., San Francisco Blinks

BY DANNY HAKIM | OCT. 1, 2019

Weeks after the city's Board of Supervisors declared the National Rifle Association a terrorist organization, the mayor clarifies that the resolution will not change city policy.

THE CITY OF San Francisco is pulling back from its face-off with the National Rifle Association, weeks after its Board of Supervisors declared the group a domestic terrorist organization. But the N.R.A. said it is not yet prepared to drop a lawsuit it filed against the city in response.

A resolution the board approved on Sept. 3 called for the city's agencies to limit their relationships with companies that do business with the N.R.A. But Mayor London Breed said in a memo on Sept. 23 that the resolution was not binding, and that it would not change the practices of city agencies. The existence of the memo was previously reported by The San Francisco Examiner.

The mayor's move came two weeks after the N.R.A. filed suit against San Francisco, alleging that the city had violated the organization's First Amendment right to free speech and was effectively moving to "blacklist anyone linked to the N.R.A."

In the memo, the mayor and the city attorney, Dennis Herrera, wrote, "The city's contracting process and policies have not changed and will not change as a result of the resolution." The notice was circulated to the heads of all city departments.

"There is an epidemic of gun violence plaguing our country, and we need to hold organizations like the N.R.A. accountable for their obstruction to real reforms to make our communities safer," Ms. Breed said in a statement on Tuesday. "While this nonbinding resolution has no force of law behind it, this doesn't take away from the fact that the N.R.A. continues to shamefully stand in the way of every single piece of gun control legislation."

TAMIR KALIFA FOR THE NEW YORK TIMES

Wayne LaPierre, the chief executive of the National Rifle Association. The group wants San Francisco to rescind or repeal its resolution declaring the group a domestic terrorist organization.

John Coté, a spokesman for Mr. Herrera, said the Sept. 23 memo was "not a concession," adding: "It just explains what has always been true — the resolution does not change the law. If the N.R.A. thinks this is a win, it's only because their lawsuit completely distorts what the resolution actually does."

William A. Brewer III, a lawyer for the N.R.A., said that city officials "wisely have attempted to pull back from what we alleged, the association alleged, was a clear violation of the association's First Amendment rights."

But the group is not ready to drop its litigation.

"What we hope is that the Board of Supervisors will further mitigate the damage they've done," he said, adding that the organization would like to see the board rescind or repeal the resolution, "or walk away from it in some binding way."

The group considered San Francisco's original declaration part of a series of actions against it by Democratic leaders in the wake of several mass shootings. The Board of Supervisors passed the resolution two days after three people were killed and 13 injured in a shooting at a garlic festival in Gilroy, Calif.

"I knew all along that this was a nonbinding resolution," Supervisor Catherine Stefani, who introduced the measure, said in a statement on Tuesday. "We made our point: The N.R.A. is a terrorist organization. I will keep fighting them using every tool at my disposal."

For now, the group is declaring victory.

"Through these actions and our public advocacy, we hope the message is now clear," Wayne LaPierre, the N.R.A.'s chief executive, said on its website on Tuesday. "The N.R.A. will always fight to protect our members and the constitutional freedoms in which they believe."

DANNY HAKIM is an investigative reporter for the business section. He has been a European economics correspondent and bureau chief in Albany and Detroit. He was also a lead reporter on the team awarded the 2009 Pulitzer Prize for Breaking News.

Watch Out, America — The Supreme Court Is Back in Session

EDITORIAL | BY THE NEW YORK TIMES | OCT. 5, 2019

And conservatives could be the big winners.

The editorial board represents the opinions of the board, its editor and the publisher. It is separate from the newsroom and the Op-Ed section.

ON MONDAY, THE Supreme Court will begin hearing cases in its first complete term since the retirement of Justice Anthony Kennedy, and the confirmation of Justice Brett Kavanaugh, gave the court a newly emboldened right-wing majority.

The current five-member bloc has already started overturning decades-old precedents and remaking the law in ways that align remarkably well with conservative policy preferences.

The new term offers no shortage of opportunities for the conservative justices to block or roll back rights for certain groups — for example, women, L.G.B.T. people and undocumented immigrants brought to America as children — while bolstering rights for others, like gun owners and those who would knock down the crumbling wall between church and state.

In one of the most hotly anticipated cases, to be argued Tuesday, the justices will consider whether employers may fire employees for being gay or transgender.

The arguments will cover three separate cases — two involving gay men who said they were fired because of their sexual orientation and one involving a transgender woman who was fired after telling her employer that she was transitioning from male to female.

Such discrimination is a daily fact of life for gay, lesbian and transgender people across the country. Some states have laws barring it, but most don't. For people in states without their own legal protections, the only hope is federal law — specifically, Title VII of the 1964 Civil Rights Act, which bars employers from firing, harassing or discriminating against an employee "because of" that person's "sex." The plaintiffs in these three cases argue that the plain language of Title VII applies to them, because they would not have been fired but for their sex — after all, if the gay men had been women, their attraction to men would not have been an issue for their employers.

The transgender woman before the court, Aimee Stephens, also argues that she was fired because she did not fit the stereotype of how a person assigned male at birth is expected to dress and act. This violates a 1989 Supreme Court ruling that Title VII bars discrimination on the basis of sex stereotypes.

The employers in these cases, with the backing of the Trump administration, say the civil rights law provides no protection to the plaintiffs, because when it was passed in the 1960s, no one imagined that it would apply to sexual orientation or gender identity. That's true — many L.G.B.T. Americans were closeted at the time, and they faced severe consequences for standing up for their equality in public. But what lawmakers might have thought more than 50 years ago is irrelevant to the matter at hand, which is what the law they passed actually says.

Cases like this are why the makeup of the Supreme Court matters so much. If Justice Kennedy were still in his seat, it's a fair bet that the plaintiffs would come out on top. Justice Kennedy wrote all of the major gay-rights opinions of the court, including Obergefell v. Hodges in 2015, which upheld a constitutional right to same-sex marriage.

Still, this should be an easy case for the conservatives, who regularly profess their allegiance to the plain language of laws. If they are nevertheless inclined to read that language narrowly, they might heed the words of their hero, Justice Antonin Scalia, who wrote the opinion for a unanimous court in 1998 that Title VII applies to cases involving harassment between members of the same sex. While Congress may not have been picturing such incidents in 1964, Justice Scalia wrote, "statutory prohibitions often go beyond the principal evil to cover reasonably comparable evils, and it is ultimately the provisions of our laws rather than the principal concerns of our legislators by which we are governed."

This term, the court also will hear a challenge to President Trump's decision in 2017 to reverse President Barack Obama's 2012 executive order protecting undocumented immigrants who were brought to the United States as children — the roughly 700,000 young men and women known as Dreamers.

Mr. Obama implemented the program, Deferred Action for Childhood Arrivals, or DACA, as a way to protect some of the most vulnerable undocumented immigrants in the nation, and he did it only after Congress repeatedly failed to pass any meaningful immigration reform. Mr. Obama claimed that he was using well-established presidential discretion to decide how to enforce immigration laws and to prioritize the deportation of certain people and not others, like the Dreamers.

This put the Trump administration in a bind. On the one hand, Mr. Trump rose to power on an anti-immigrant platform, and his supporters are hungry to see him carry that out. (He's also eager to erase every accomplishment of Mr. Obama's.) On the other hand, the Dreamers are a sympathetic group of young people, as Mr. Trump has acknowledged, and Americans broadly support their being able to stay in the only country that many of them have ever really known.

Had Mr. Trump simply said that he was rescinding DACA because he did not think it was a wise policy, he would have been on firmer legal ground. But because he was afraid of taking responsibility for destroying the Dreamers' lives, Mr. Trump is trying to pass the job off to the Supreme Court by arguing that DACA was an illegal exercise of authority from the start.

That's simply wrong — not to mention suspicious coming from an administration that claims to have broad authority in other immigration contexts. It also makes the case harder for Mr. Trump at the Supreme Court because he did not adequately explain his reasoning,

ILLUSTRATION BY THE NEW YORK TIMES; PHOTOGRAPH BY GABRIELLA DEMCZUK FOR THE NEW YORK TIMES

as is required when reversing a previous administration's position. When the justices hear this case in November, they ought to tell the president that if he wants to kill off a popular program, he'll need to look the American people in the eye and own it.

The way the justices handle two other high-profile cases — on guns and abortion — could reveal just how far and fast the court's new conservative majority is willing to go to implement its vision for America.

In January, the justices agreed to hear a gun-rights case for the first time in a decade. The lawsuit is a challenge to a New York City law limiting gun owners' ability to transport guns outside their home. With five justices who are solidly in favor of gun owners' rights, the outcome would seem nearly preordained.

It might not be, however. After the court agreed to hear the case, New York City threw out the challenged law. Normally, this means that the case is, in legal jargon, moot: The plaintiffs got what they were asking for, so there's no longer any dispute for a court to resolve.

But once again, court personnel matters. If Justice Kennedy were still on the bench, there's a good chance that the court would not have taken this case at all. It's a different story with Justice Kavanaugh, whose work as a federal appeals court judge suggests he is even more protective of the Second Amendment than was Justice Scalia, who wrote the landmark 2008 ruling that guaranteed an individual right to keep and bear arms.

Last but not least is abortion rights — in the form of the first case involving the perennial hot-button issue to reach the Supreme Court since President Trump's two nominees were confirmed. On Friday, the justices agreed to hear a case out of Louisiana, which enacted a law in 2014 requiring that doctors who perform abortions have admitting privileges at a hospital within 30 miles of where the terminations are performed.

Wait, you might be thinking: Isn't this the same issue the court decided just three years ago, when it struck down parts of a nearly identical law in Texas as a sham policy intended to make it much more difficult for a woman to exercise her constitutional right to choose? Yes, it is. In that 2016 case, Justice Kennedy joined the court's four liberals to strike down parts of the Texas law. This should have been enough to keep the Louisiana case from getting anywhere near the Supreme Court. But the notoriously conservative United States Court of Appeals for the Fifth Circuit upheld the Louisiana law anyway, and for a simple reason: With Justice Kennedy gone, the anti-abortion crusaders and their sympathizers on the federal bench feel that their moment has finally arrived.

They are right. Even if the court reverses the Fifth Circuit and prevents the Louisiana law from taking effect, as it clearly should, there are now five Supreme Court justices who are hostile to women's reproductive rights. And even though an enduring majority of Americans support keeping abortion legal, the path to overturning Roe v. Wade — the conservative movement's single biggest target over the past half century — is clearer than ever.

Supreme Court to Weigh Taking Bellwether Case Against Gun Industry

BY KRISTIN HUSSEY AND ELIZABETH WILLIAMSON

PUBLISHED NOV. 5, 2019 | UPDATED NOV. 12, 2019

A suit by Sandy Hook families against Remington, the maker of the AR-15-style rifle used in the massacre, tries to test a law shielding the firearms industry from liability.

THE SUPREME COURT will consider this week whether to hear a case seeking to pierce firearm manufacturers' legal immunity in the aftermath of shootings.

The case, Remington Arms Co. v. Soto, pits relatives of those killed in the Sandy Hook Elementary School shooting against Remington, the maker of the AR-15-style rifle used in the Dec. 14, 2012, massacre in Newtown, Conn. Twenty first graders and six educators died.

The lawsuit challenges a 2005 law protecting gun makers from legal liability when their weapons are used in crimes. The families argue that Remington violated Connecticut's Unfair Trade Practices Act by recklessly marketing the rifle to disturbed young men like the Sandy Hook gunman through product placement in violent video games and advertising pitches like "consider your man card reissued."

Most attention in the current Supreme Court term has been on whether the justices will expand Second Amendment rights. But should they allow the case to move forward to trial, either by refusing to hear Remington's appeal or by hearing the case and ruling in the families' favor, the lawsuit could provide a legal road map for victims and survivors seeking to hold gun makers accountable for gun violence.

The justices will meet on Friday to discuss whether to take the case. The court may grant or deny review shortly afterward, or continue considering the matter.

The appeal was brought by Remington after the Connecticut Supreme Court allowed the lawsuit to proceed to trial. Remington says the families' case, if successful, would "eviscerate" the 2005 federal law.

The National Rifle Association, the Connecticut Citizens Defense League, Second Amendment law professors, nine states and 22 members of the House are among the signatories of a half-dozen legal briefs supporting Remington. The N.R.A. argued that the families' challenge to the 2005 law could open the door to other lawsuits, potentially putting the firearm industry "out of business by unlimited and uncertain liability for criminal misuse of their products."

Remington said in a legal filing that the Connecticut lawsuit was "widely recognized as a bellwether for the future of firearms litigation nationwide."

The Connecticut Supreme Court agreed with a lower court judge that one element of the case cannot be tried, saying that the federal shield law precluded the families' argument that Remington had "negligently entrusted" a weapon of war to an untrained civilian population.

But in a 4-to-3 ruling, the Connecticut justices upheld another element of the families' case, saying the lawsuit could continue to trial under the state consumer protection law. "Connecticut law does not permit advertisements that promote or encourage violent, criminal behavior," the decision said.

The lawsuit, filed in 2014 by the families of nine victims and a teacher who was shot and survived, accuses Remington of using militaristic and hypermasculine advertising for its Bushmaster AR-15-style rifle in order to attract disturbed young men like the Sandy Hook killer. On its website, Bushmaster advertised the rifle with the "man card" slogan and the tagline, "If it's good enough for the military, it's good enough for you."

The 2005 federal law, called the Protection of Lawful Commerce in Arms Act, was the culmination of an extended effort by the

National Rifle Association to create a blanket protection for gun companies from most liability lawsuits. When the bill passed, the organization noted its seven-year campaign for the law, including "a comprehensive legislative and election strategy," according to its chief lobbyist.

At the time, the firearms industry and President George W. Bush, who signed the law, said it was necessary to protect gun makers from "frivolous lawsuits" that could bankrupt the companies. Wayne LaPierre, the chief executive of the National Rifle Association, called the law "historic," saying its passage by Congress was the industry's most significant legislative victory in 20 years.

Critics, including scores of law professors who signed a letter to Congress protesting the bill in 2005, have said the law extends protection to the firearms industry that few other industries enjoy.

Several previous legal challenges to the shield law have failed, but the Sandy Hook case is the first to take on the industry in this way, said Adam Winkler, a constitutional law expert at the U.C.L.A. School of Law who has written about gun rights.

The nearly five years that the Sandy Hook case has spent winding through the court system "shows you how strong this immunity really is," Mr. Winkler said.

The federal law includes six narrow exceptions under which plaintiffs can sue gun companies, including if they can prove they were harmed after a manufacturer "knowingly violated a state or federal statute applicable to the sale or marketing of the product."

The Connecticut Supreme Court's decision "made a pretty persuasive case that the advertising fit into this exception," Mr. Winkler said.

The Connecticut state court ruling brought the case closer to the discovery phase, a pretrial exchange of information between the parties. The Newtown families have asked for internal Remington documents, emails and other communications to "pull back the curtain" on the company's marketing practices, the families and their lawyers have said.

Public sentiment toward other industries, including tobacco and pharmaceutical, have shifted significantly after documents revealed during the discovery phase of legal cases showed that the companies misled the American public.

ELIZABETH WILLIAMSON is a feature writer based in the Washington bureau. She previously worked for The Wall Street Journal and The Washington Post, and was a foreign correspondent for a decade, covering Central and Eastern Europe.

Second Amendment Case May Fizzle Out at the Supreme Court

BY ADAM LIPTAK | DEC. 2, 2019

Arguments in the court's first case on the scope of the amendment in nearly a decade focused on whether the repeal of a New York law made the case moot.

WASHINGTON — The Supreme Court's first Second Amendment case in nearly a decade may not result in a ruling of any particular consequence, judging from questioning at arguments on Monday that focused largely on whether the repeal of a New York City law made the case challenging it moot.

"What's left of this case?" Justice Ruth Bader Ginsburg asked. "The petitioners have gotten all the relief that they sought."

The other three members of the court's liberal wing made similar points. "The other side has thrown in the towel," Justice Sonia Sotomayor told a lawyer for the challengers. "You're asking us to opine on a law that's not on the books anymore."

Chief Justice John G. Roberts Jr., a member of the court's conservative majority, asked questions that seemed aimed at making sure that the case was truly moot. But two other conservatives, Justices Samuel A. Alito Jr. and Neil M. Gorsuch, appeared ready to decide the case, saying that the repeal of the law did not settle every question before the court.

Justice Gorsuch said he was skeptical of the city's "herculean, late-breaking efforts to moot the case."

Justices Clarence Thomas and Brett M. Kavanaugh asked no questions.

The law had limited city residents who had "premises licenses" from transporting their guns outside their homes. It allowed them to take their guns to one of seven shooting ranges within the city limits, but it barred them from taking their guns anywhere else, including second homes and shooting ranges outside the city, even when the guns were unloaded and locked in a container separate from any ammunition.

Three city residents and the New York State Rifle and Pistol Association sued to challenge the law but lost in Federal District Court in Manhattan and in the United States Court of Appeals for the Second Circuit. A unanimous three-judge panel of the Second Circuit ruled that the ordinance passed constitutional muster.

After the Supreme Court granted review, the city repealed its law, apparently fearful of a loss that could sweep away other gun control regulations, too. For good measure, New York State enacted a law allowing people with premises licenses to take their guns to their homes and businesses and to shooting ranges and competitions, whether in the city or not.

Even the court's more liberal members indicated that the repealed law would be problematic were it properly before the court.

"One problem with the prior regulation," Justice Ginsburg said, was that "if you wanted to have a gun in your second home, you had to buy a second gun."

"And what public safety or any other reasonable end is served by saying you have to have two guns instead of one — and one of those guns has to be maintained in a place that is often unoccupied and that, therefore, more vulnerable to theft?" she continued.

Paul D. Clement, a lawyer for the challengers in the case, New York State Rifle and Pistol Association v. City of New York, No. 18-280, said the restrictions imposed by the ordinance were at odds with the words of the Second Amendment.

"The Second Amendment protects rights to keep and bear arms," he said. "That latter right makes clear that the Second Amendment protects rights that are not strictly limited to the premises."

Mr. Clement's efforts to keep the argument focused on whether the repealed law was constitutional mostly failed. He was instead peppered with questions about whether the case was moot.

In response, he questioned a requirement in the city's replacement law that the transport of guns to permissible places be "continuous and uninterrupted."

Mr. Clement said his clients were entitled to a clear judicial determination of whether they would violate the new law if they stopped for coffee or a bathroom break on their way to a shooting range or a second home. That theory seemed to satisfy Justice Gorsuch as a ground on which to say the case was not moot.

"Why isn't that good enough?" he asked. If under both the old law and the new one the challengers could not "take their firearms locked safely to a range and stop along the way for a cup of coffee or a bathroom break," Justice Gorsuch said, there would seem to be a live controversy.

But Jeffrey B. Wall, a lawyer for the federal government who was arguing on behalf of the challengers, declined to endorse that argument for keeping the case alive. "It's a close call," he said, before adding, "In our view, that's a new controversy that arises from the new law, not the old controversy in the old law."

For his part, Richard P. Dearing, a lawyer for the city, said that coffee stops and bathroom breaks "are entirely permissible" under the new law.

Justice Alito asked whether one of the plaintiffs "could stop to visit his mother for a couple of hours to take care of a few things for her" while transporting firearms.

Mr. Dearing said that question should be resolved in a fresh challenge to the new law.

Mr. Wall, the lawyer for the federal government, said the case was not moot for a different reason, because the plaintiffs may still be entitled to monetary damages from the city.

Mr. Clement's response to that theory was lukewarm. "We did not make a specific request for damages below," he said. "I'm happy to affirm that we'd like damages."

Chief Justice Roberts asked just two questions, each seemingly intended to elicit concessions from Mr. Dearing that could allow the court to rule that the case was moot. The chief justice first asked whether the challengers could suffer negative consequences for what was unlawful conduct while the city law was in place.

"Is there any way in which any violation could prejudice a gun owner?" the chief justice asked about the old law. Mr. Dearing said no.

The chief justice then asked whether a ruling that the case was moot would stop a further lawsuit for money. Mr. Dearing said no, so long as such a lawsuit was timely and otherwise proper.

Chief Justice Roberts's questions were hardly conclusive evidence of his position, but they suggested that he was thinking about how to draft an opinion ruling the case was moot.

The larger question in the case, one the court may not address, is whether lower courts have been faithfully applying its key precedent, District of Columbia v. Heller, which was decided by a 5-to-4 vote in 2008. The decision revolutionized Second Amendment jurisprudence by identifying an individual right to own guns, but it ruled only that the right applied inside the home, for self-defense.

Proponents of gun rights have been frustrated by lower-court rulings that have generally upheld various kinds of gun control laws, often relying on a passage in the Heller decision that said some restrictions were presumptively constitutional.

"Nothing in our opinion," Justice Antonin Scalia wrote for the majority in a passage that was apparently the price of Justice Anthony M. Kennedy's fifth vote, "should be taken to cast doubt on longstanding prohibitions on the possession of firearms by felons and the mentally ill, or laws forbidding the carrying of firearms in sensitive places such as schools and government buildings, or laws imposing conditions and qualifications on the commercial sale of arms."

Justice Scalia died in 2016, and Justice Kennedy retired last year.

Mr. Clement urged the justices to decide the case on the merits. That would "send a very important signal to the lower courts," he said, that some gun regulations are "unconstitutional, full stop."

ADAM LIPTAK covers the Supreme Court and writes Sidebar, a column on legal developments. A graduate of Yale Law School, he practiced law for 14 years before joining The Times in 2002.

CHAPTER 2

Violence and More Violence

There is no shortage of media coverage of tragic public shootings, from the massacre of children in Newtown, Conn., to the terror faced by young adults at a high school in Parkland, Fla. In both instances, the young male shooters had troubled backgrounds and serious mental illnesses. While many argue for gun control, another segment of the population pushes back against them, arguing that the overwhelming majority of gun owners are law-abiding citizens. Gun ownership represents a lifestyle to many of these owners.

Nation Reels After Gunman Massacres 20 Children at School in Connecticut

BY JAMES BARRON | DEC. 14, 2012

A 20-YEAR-OLD MAN wearing combat gear and armed with semiautomatic pistols and a semiautomatic rifle killed 26 people — 20 of them children — in an attack in an elementary school in central Connecticut on Friday. Witnesses and officials described a horrific scene as the gunman, with brutal efficiency, chose his victims in two classrooms while other students dove under desks and hid in closets.

Hundreds of terrified parents arrived as their sobbing children were led out of the Sandy Hook Elementary School in a wooded corner of Newtown, Conn. By then, all of the victims had been shot and most were dead, and the gunman, identified as Adam Lanza, had committed suicide. The children killed were said to be 5 to 10 years old.

A 28th person, found dead in a house in the town, was also believed to have been shot by Mr. Lanza. That victim, one law enforcement official said, was Mr. Lanza's mother, Nancy Lanza, who was initially reported to be a teacher at the school. She apparently owned the guns he used.

Although reports at the time indicated that the principal of the school let Mr. Lanza in because she recognized him, his mother did not work at the school, and he shot his way in, defeating a security system requiring visitors to be buzzed in. Moments later, the principal was shot dead when she went to investigate the sound of gunshots. The school psychologist was also among those who died.

The rampage, coming less than two weeks before Christmas, was the nation's second-deadliest school shooting, exceeded only by the 2007 Virginia Tech massacre, in which a gunman killed 32 people and then himself.

Law enforcement officials said Mr. Lanza had grown up in Newtown, and he was remembered by high school classmates as smart, introverted and nervous. They said he had gone out of his way not to attract attention when he was younger.

The gunman was chillingly accurate. A spokesman for the State Police said he left only one wounded survivor at the school. All the others hit by the barrage of bullets from the guns Mr. Lanza carried died, suggesting that they were shot at point-blank range. One law enforcement official said the shootings occurred in two classrooms in a section of the single-story Sandy Hook Elementary School.

Some who were there said the shooting occurred during morning announcements, and the initial shots could be heard over the school's public address system. The bodies of those killed were still in the school as of 10 p.m. Friday.

The New York City medical examiner's office sent a "portable morgue" to Newtown to help with the aftermath of the shootings, a spokeswoman, Ellen Borakove, confirmed late Friday.

RICHARD PERRY/THE NEW YORK TIMES

In Newtown, Conn., where a gunman killed 26 people at an elementary school, a memorial service at St. Rose of Lima Church drew the grieving.

Law enforcement officials offered no hint of what had motivated Mr. Lanza. It was also unclear, one investigator said, why Mr. Lanza — after shooting his mother to death inside her home — drove her car to the school and slaughtered the children. "I don't think anyone knows the answers to those questions at this point," the official said. As for a possible motive, he added, "we don't know much for sure."

F.B.I. agents interviewed his brother, Ryan Lanza, in Hoboken, N.J. His father, Peter Lanza, who was divorced from Nancy Lanza, was also questioned, one official said.

Newtown, a postcard-perfect New England town where everyone seems to know everyone else and where there had lately been holiday tree lightings with apple cider and hot chocolate, was plunged into mourning. Stunned residents attended four memorial services in the town on Friday evening as detectives continued the search for clues, and an explanation.

RICHARD PERRY/THE NEW YORK TIMES

People listened to the memorial through the windows at St. Rose of Lima Church, one of several churches in town conducting services.

Maureen Kerins, a hospital nurse who lives close to the school, learned of the shooting from television and hurried to the school to see if she could help.

"I stood outside waiting to go in, but a police officer came out and said they didn't need any nurses," she said, "so I knew it wasn't good."

In the cold light of Friday morning, faces told the story outside the stricken school. There were the frightened faces of children who were crying as they were led out in a line. There were the grim faces of women. There were the relieved-looking faces of a couple and their little girl.

The shootings set off a tide of anguish nationwide. In Illinois and Georgia, flags were lowered to half-staff in memory of the victims. And at the White House, President Obama struggled to read a statement in the White House briefing room. More than once, he dabbed his eyes.

LUKE SHARRETT FOR THE NEW YORK TIMES

President Obama spoke about the shootings at Sandy Hook Elementary School in Newtown.

"Our hearts are broken," Mr. Obama said, adding that his first reaction was not as a president, but as a parent.

"I know there is not a parent in America who does not feel the same overwhelming grief that I do," he said.

He called the victims "beautiful little kids."

"They had their entire lives ahead of them: birthdays, graduations, weddings, kids of their own," he said. Then the president reached up to the corner of one eye.

Mr. Obama called for "meaningful action" to stop such shootings, but he did not spell out details. In his nearly four years in office, he has not pressed for expanded gun control. But he did allude on Friday to a desire to have politicians put aside their differences to deal with ways to prevent future shootings.

Gov. Dannel P. Malloy of Connecticut, who went to Newtown, called the shootings "a tragedy of unspeakable terms."

"Evil visited this community today," he said.

Lt. J. Paul Vance, a spokesman for the Connecticut State Police, described "a very horrific and difficult scene" at the school, which had 700 students in kindergarten through fourth grade. It had a security protocol that called for doors to be locked during the day and visitors to be checked on a video monitor inside.

"You had to buzz in and out and the whole nine yards," said a former chairwoman of the Newtown board of education, Lillian Bittman. "When you buzz, you come up on our screen."

The lock system did not go into effect until 9:30 each morning, according to a letter to parents from the principal, Dawn Hochsprung, that was posted on several news Web sites. The letter was apparently written earlier in the school year.

Lieutenant Vance said the Newtown police had called for help from police departments nearby and began a manhunt, checking "every nook and cranny and every room."

Officers were seen kicking in doors as they worked their way through the school.

Lieutenant Vance said the students who died had been in two classrooms. Others said that as the horror unfolded, students and teachers tried to hide in places the gunman would not think to look. Teachers locked the doors, turned off the lights and closed the blinds. Some ordered students to duck under their desks.

The teachers did not explain what was going on, but they did not have to. Everyone could hear the gunfire.

Yvonne Cech, a school librarian, said she had spent 45 minutes locked in a closet with two library clerks, a library catalog assistant and 18 fourth graders.

"The SWAT team escorted us out," she said, and then the children were reunited with their parents.

Lieutenant Vance said 18 youngsters were pronounced dead at the school and two others were taken to hospitals, where they were declared dead. All the adults who were killed at the school were pronounced dead there.

Law enforcement officials said the weapons used by the gunman were a Sig Sauer and a Glock, both handguns. The police also found a Bushmaster .223 M4 carbine.

One law enforcement official said the guns had not been traced because they had not yet been removed from the school, but state licensing records or permits apparently indicated that Ms. Lanza owned weapons of the same makes and models.

"He visited two classrooms," said a law enforcement official at the scene, adding that those two classrooms were adjoining.

The first 911 call was recorded about 9:30 and said someone had been shot at the school, an almost unthinkable turn of events on what had begun as just another chilly day in quiet Newtown. Soon, frantic parents were racing to the school, hoping their children were all right. By 10:30, the shooting had stopped. By then, the police had arrived with dogs.

"There is going to be a black cloud over this area forever," said Craig Ansman, who led his 4-year-old daughter from the preschool down the street from the elementary school. "It will never go away."

Reporting on the Connecticut shootings was contributed by **AL BAKER, CHARLES V. BAGLI, SUSAN BEACHY, JACK BEGG, DAVID W. CHEN, ALISON LEIGH COWAN, ROBERT DAVEY, MATT FLEGENHEIMER, JOSEPH GOLDSTEIN, EMMARIE HUETTEMAN, KRISTIN HUSSEY, THOMAS KAPLAN, ELIZABETH MAKER, PATRICK MCGEEHAN, SHEELAGH MCNEILL, MICHAEL MOSS, ANDY NEWMAN, RICHARD PÉREZ-PEÑA, JENNIFER PRESTON, WILLIAM K. RASHBAUM, MOTOKO RICH, RAY RIVERA, LIZ ROBBINS, EMILY S. RUEB, ERIC SCHMITT, MICHAEL SCHWIRTZ, KIRK SEMPLE, WENDY RUDERMAN, JONATHAN WEISMAN, VIVIAN YEE** and **KATE ZERNIKE**.

Adam Lanza's Mental Problems 'Completely Untreated' Before Newtown Shootings, Report Says

BY ALISON LEIGH COWAN | NOV. 21, 2014

MEDICAL EXPERTS AT Yale University had called for drastic measures to help Adam Lanza in the years before he shot and killed 26 people at Sandy Hook Elementary School in Newtown, Conn., but those calls "went largely unheeded" by his mother, who was also shot to death, according to a new study.

The report, based on a comprehensive examination of the medical and school histories of Mr. Lanza, 20, found he was "completely untreated in the years before the shooting" for psychiatric and physical ailments like anxiety and obsessive-compulsive disorder, and was also deprived of recommended services and drugs.

The report also stated that undiagnosed anorexia could have affected his mental state.

The most recent of many inquiries into the events that led up to the massacre in December 2012, the report is the first to delve into Mr. Lanza's medical history in detail and examine efforts to help him in the months and years before the shootings. It relied heavily on subpoenaed medical records, emails and other information obtained with the help of Mr. Lanza's father, Peter.

Mr. Lanza's mother, Nancy, his main caregiver after she and his father separated, was fatally shot by her son minutes before he arrived at the school and killed 20 schoolchildren and six staff members. He then killed himself.

The 114-page report, produced by a panel convened by the state's Office of the Child Advocate, did not find direct fault with those in Mr. Lanza's life for the violence, but it did conclude that his mother had sought to appease her son and was inclined to accommodate his disabilities rather than treat them.

That was true even later in his life, when he showed signs of "severe and deteriorating internalized mental health problems" and was still allowed to "retain access to numerous firearms and high-capacity magazines" in his home, the report said.

After consulting Yale University's Child Study Center when her son was in the ninth grade, Ms. Lanza resisted its recommendation that he take medication for some of his problems. The report also concluded that Yale's recommendations "for extensive special education supports, ongoing expert consultation and rigorous therapeutic supports" also "went largely unheeded."

"It's not that his mental illness was a predisposing factor in this tragedy," Dr. Harold Schwartz, chief psychiatrist at Hartford Hospital's Institute of Living, said at a news conference held on Friday to discuss the report, of which he was an author. "It was his untreated mental illness that was a predisposing factor."

Allowing ailments that are responsive to medication to go untreated and resisting other kinds of emotional support were missed chances for the parents to help their son, added Dr. Julian Ford, an author of the report and director of the University of Connecticut's Center for Trauma Recovery and Juvenile Justice.

"The Yale team offered a comprehensive approach," Dr. Ford said. But, he said, "the family pulled away from that and did not work with the team in part because Mrs. Lanza did not think that was possible for Adam and she wanted to keep Adam sheltered."

Another complication noted in the report was Adam Lanza's anorexia, diagnosed only after his death, when the coroner determined he was 6 feet tall and weighed only 112 pounds. Authors of the report said anorexia could lead to malnutrition and cognitive impairment and cited Mr. Lanza's obsessive workouts with "Dance, Dance Revolution," which left him drenched in sweat. "He was so deeply troubled," Dr. Ford said during the news conference. "That led him to take some extreme measures in which he was acting like his own body ceased to exist. So he was disconnected, not just from other people, but from his own body."

In Connecticut, the Office of the Child Advocate has a mandate to "conduct investigations of child fatalities and issue public reports with the particular focus on preventing future child deaths."

The report also faulted the school system for not doing a better job of monitoring Mr. Lanza's progress, educationally and emotionally, each time he was allowed to receive his education in a "homebound" environment because of difficulties he had in social settings.

The bubblelike environment at home only heightened his sense of isolation, the authors found, and ultimately made him more prone to the violence he fantasized about in an online community for mass-murder enthusiasts. "He was losing a sense of other people as human beings," Dr. Ford surmised.

The authors also questioned whether Mr. Lanza's privileged upbringing had helped him fall between the cracks. The report did not offer an answer.

With Florida Shooting Survivors, N.R.A. Spokeswoman Holds Back. With Conservatives, It's a Different Story.

BY DANIEL VICTOR | FEB. 22, 2018

DANA LOESCH, THE spokeswoman for the National Rifle Association, focused her ire on the news media in a combative and defiant speech on Thursday, in sharp contrast to the approach she took before an audience of gun violence survivors a day earlier.

In a speech at the Conservative Political Action Conference in Oxon Hill, Md., Ms. Loesch accused the news media of ignoring the N.R.A.'s viewpoint and cashing in on the deaths of students.

"Many in legacy media love mass shootings," Ms. Loesch said. "You guys love it. I'm not saying that you love the tragedy, but I am saying that you love the ratings. Crying white mothers are ratings gold."

The gun lobbying organization, which went silent on its Twitter account for six days following the shooting that killed 17 people at Marjory Stoneman Douglas High School in Florida, has waded back into the national conversation over guns and school safety.

In his speech at the conference, Wayne LaPierre, the group's president, slammed "the breakneck speed of calls for more gun control, and the breathless national media eager to smear the N.R.A."

"As usual, the opportunists wasted not one second to exploit tragedy for political gain," he said.

The remarks came one day after Ms. Loesch and Senator Marco Rubio, Republican of Florida, were heavily jeered at a CNN town hall-style meeting that was attended by many of the families affected by last week's school shooting. There, Ms. Loesch didn't change the substance of her arguments or make concessions, but she resisted many of her common lines of attack.

“I don’t believe that this insane monster should have ever been able to obtain a firearm, ever,” she said. “I do not think that he should have gotten his hands on any kind of weapon. That’s No. 1.”

She spoke in a somewhat measured tone and praised the students for using their voices. She said that the system for background checks was “flawed” (though the N.R.A. opposes their expansion).

The crowd, which overwhelmingly supported gun control, chanted “shame on you” as she left the stage.

On Thursday, Ms. Loesch said she had needed a security detail to leave the event.

“There were people rushing the stage and screaming, ‘Burn her,’ ” she said.

A CNN spokesman said that its security personnel accompanied all the speakers, including Ms. Loesch, from the stage, and that Ms. Loesch also had her own private security. But he did not say whether she had been threatened.

The N.R.A. criticizing the media is nothing new, but some journalists chafed at the idea that they were emotionally untouched by the deaths of children.

How Sandy Hook Families Hope to Pierce the Gun Industry's Legal Shield

BY RICK ROJAS AND KRISTIN HUSSEY | APRIL 8, 2019

DOCUMENTS PROVED THERE were cover-ups: The industry knew about the dangers, but hid facts from consumers, and millions of pages described false advertising and suppressed scientific research. The details, once surfaced, not only revealed wrongdoing but changed public perception.

Lawsuits against cigarette manufacturers exposed crucial confidential records and completely transformed the tobacco industry.

Now, families of the victims from the massacre at Sandy Hook Elementary School hope to replicate the tactic: using litigation as a means to pry open the gun industry, employing the discovery process to unearth internal communications and examine the practices behind marketing and selling powerful firearms like the one used in the attack.

"We can find out what the Remington defendants have tried every step of the way to block in discovery," said David Wheeler, whose 6-year-old son, Ben, died at Sandy Hook, about the gun maker that was among the companies named in the lawsuit.

Joshua D. Koskoff, a lawyer for the families, described the discovery stage as "really the most important thing we've been waiting to do."

The ruling last month — allowing the families to maneuver around the vast federal protections shielding the gun industry from some lawsuits — arrived more than six years after the gunman stormed into the elementary school in Newtown, Conn., killing 26 people, including 20 first graders.

Gun companies are protected from most legal action when their weapons are used to commit a crime, as stipulated by Congress in 2005. The families tested a novel strategy to pierce those protections by focusing on the marketing for the AR-15-style Bushmaster used by the gunman in the attack.

In the lawsuit, the families assert that the weapon used in the massacre was marketed in a way — with militaristic and hypermasculine slogans — that specifically reached out to troubled young men like the one who carried out the attack.

The families' aim, according to past legal filings, is to compel the companies to turn over troves of documents in hope that the records will bolster the case, like those discussing strategies for branding and promoting the weapon, including product placements in video games and marketing it as a good gift for family members.

Financial documents filed by Remington with the Securities and Exchange Commission show that increasing sales of the Bushmaster AR-style rifles was one of the company's highest priorities in 2009. That year, a Remington executive's bonus was tied to implementing a plan for the company to hit specific sales targets for the Bushmaster weapon like the one legally purchased by the gunman's mother. The executive exceeded the company's target for 2009.

The recent court decision offered a moment of triumph for the Newtown families, who still face new struggles and daily reminders of their loss. Newtown was shaken again by the recent suicide of Jeremy Richman, whose 6-year-old daughter, Avielle, was among the Sandy Hook victims.

It remains unknown exactly what records will be excavated in the Sandy Hook case, but hundreds of miles away in Florida, Fred Guttenberg took notice.

He is pursuing his own legal action, in his case against the parent company of Smith & Wesson, which made the weapon used in the attack at the Parkland, Fla., high school where his 14-year-old daughter, Jaime, was killed.

The development in Connecticut has emboldened him in his own effort.

"They're concerned and they should be concerned," Mr. Guttenberg, whose daughter was one of 17 people killed at Marjory Stoneman Douglas High School, said of the gun industry.

MONICA JORGE FOR THE NEW YORK TIMES

David Wheeler's 6-year-old son, Ben, died in the mass shooting at Sandy Hook Elementary School.

By bringing a lawsuit against the companies that manufactured and sold the weapon used by the gunman, legal experts said, the families were pursuing a familiar strategy that had led to the revelation in other industries — the tobacco business, car manufacturers and pharmaceutical companies — of dishonest practices and a disregard for the well-being of customers and the public.

"There are just so many product liability cases that have unfolded in similar ways," said Carl Tobias, a law professor at the University of Richmond. "They dug and dug and dug and found out what actually happened," he added. "Discovery is the tool."

Remington and the other companies named in the lawsuit, along with others in the gun industry, have mounted a vigorous defense.

They counter that federal law shields the companies from these kinds of claims when their weapons are used in a crime. Remington has asked the state court to delay any ruling in anticipation of an expected appeal to the United States Supreme Court.

Lawyers for the gun companies did not respond to requests for comment.

The discovery process is a portion of the case where lawyers amass evidence, drawing from depositions with the sworn testimony of executives, experts and others, written questionnaires submitted to the other side and documents that the opposing side is compelled to turn over.

The volume of lawsuits against tobacco companies prompted the release of documents — from the discovery process during suits as well as disclosures from corporate whistle-blowers — that showed the companies had known far more than they had publicly acknowledged about the harmful effects of their products and the addictive nature of nicotine. The information led to a shift in society's impressions of tobacco.

Now, large volumes of documents about cigarette companies are available online; one archive maintained by the University of California San Francisco has 90,111,026 pages, much of it coming from lawsuits.

"It stripped away all credibility of anything the industry might say," said Matthew L. Myers, the president of the Campaign for Tobacco-Free Kids and a leading figure in the litigation against tobacco companies.

But just as other plaintiffs have drawn lessons from tobacco litigation, so have other industries. Mr. Myers said it was very likely that the gun companies had studied the tobacco companies' shortcomings.

"What became clear from the tobacco industry documents: There was a brazenness in believing they could keep these documents from the public eye," Mr. Myers said. "They wrote down things that careful people would not write down."

The Sandy Hook gun lawsuit has attracted intense interest because, unlike other legal battles over weapons, it has not been clobbered by the protections enshrined in federal law.

TOM BRENNER/THE NEW YORK TIMES

Fred Guttenberg is pursuing legal action against the gun company that manufactured the weapon used in the attack at the Parkland, Fla., high school where his daughter was killed.

In a 4-to-3 ruling, the Connecticut Supreme Court agreed with a lower court judge's decision to dismiss most of the families' claims, yet also found that federal law did not prevent the families from bringing a lawsuit based on wrongful marketing claims under Connecticut state law.

The National Shooting Sports Foundation, a trade association representing the firearm industry, said the ruling was "at odds with all other state and federal appellate courts that have interpreted the scope" of the federal protections.

Scott Wilson, president of the Connecticut Citizens Defense League, a Second Amendment rights organization, criticized the ruling. "I think it's a miscarriage of justice," he said. He also disputed the depiction of the semiautomatic rifle as a combat weapon too dangerous or complicated for civilians.

But advocates of gun control and others welcomed the ruling as an indication that the federal protections were not impenetrable.

"Any industry needs robust oversight," said Alla Lefkowitz, the deputy director of affirmative litigation at Everytown for Gun Safety, an organization that advocates stricter gun measures. "I'm not aware of any other industry that has this kind of protection and I think it's particularly inappropriate for any kind of industry to have this kind of protection."

The victory is not clear cut. The case has languished for years in court; legal experts believe it is still years from being resolved, and could likely return to the State Supreme Court and even advance to the United States Supreme Court.

Still, Mr. Guttenberg was forward-looking. "We're not going to continue being victims," he said. "We're going to fight. We're going to get this somehow or another fixed."

Newtown Wasn't an End for Gun Control. It Was a Beginning.

BY MAGGIE ASTOR | APRIL 29, 2019

NEWTOWN, CONN. — Six years ago this month, Mark Barden and Nicole Hockley watched from the gallery, counting the yeas, as the Senate voted on expanding background checks.

Four months had passed since his son, Daniel, and her son, Dylan, were killed at Sandy Hook Elementary School, and at no point in that time had they imagined the bill would fail. The assault weapons ban the Senate rejected the same day was one thing, but background checks seemed like "low-hanging fruit," Ms. Hockley said.

The bill failed.

Afterward, standing by President Barack Obama at a news conference in the Rose Garden, Ms. Hockley focused all her energy on not bursting into tears. Mr. Barden looked at his wife, Jackie, and their two surviving children and thought: "I've failed you. Your country has failed you."

To many people who thought the massacre of 20 first graders and six of their educators would fundamentally change the nation's gun politics, the loss felt irrecoverable. But those votes in April 2013 turned out to be a beginning, not an end.

They led to new activism and organizations and fresh approaches to the gun control debate, and they helped motivate gun control advocates like Michael R. Bloomberg, who brought more money and visibility to the cause. Those groups, in turn, provided critical resources for the survivors, family members and activists galvanized by the shooting at Marjory Stoneman Douglas High School in Parkland, Fla., in February 2018.

Now, as the National Rifle Association struggles with internal battles, gun issues figure prominently in presidential politics, and mass shootings like Saturday's assault at a California synagogue continue on a regular basis, the influence of the Sandy Hook activism is a sharp reminder that federal inaction on issues like guns is seldom a final word. Instead, movement on gun violence and other social issues is often a long, slow process that builds on failures as well as successes.

"There was logic to the idea that if Sandy Hook didn't create an epiphany in this country, what will?" said Senator Christopher S. Murphy of Connecticut, one of Congress's most vocal proponents of stricter gun laws. "But that's not how politics works. There are almost no epiphany moments in American politics. You have to build your power, and we had none of it."

Gun policy continues to be deeply divisive, and there remains a highly motivated portion of the electorate who not only oppose gun restrictions but vote on that issue above any other. N.R.A.-backed candidates did particularly well in Florida in November, despite it being the epicenter of the March for Our Lives movement. Three new states this year have enacted laws that allow residents to carry firearms without a permit or license, and numerous other expansions of gun rights were passed at the state level in the years between Newtown and Parkland.

"People on our side haven't shifted away from their positions," said Alan Gottlieb, executive vice president of the Second Amendment Foundation.

This was evident in the full-throated defense of gun rights at the N.R.A.'s annual convention this past weekend. Still, as polls have shown growing support for a wide range of restrictions, there has been a corresponding shift in the focus of the arguments against those restrictions.

For instance, the N.R.A. and some other groups say that on principle, they don't oppose red-flag laws, which allow the removal of firearms from people judged to pose an imminent threat. The problem, they argue, is a lack of due process protections in individual proposals. This has caused a growing rift between the N.R.A. and smaller groups to its right that advertise themselves as uncompromising.

MARCUS YAM FOR THE NEW YORK TIMES

A memorial at the entrance of Sandy Hook Elementary School in Newtown, Conn., where 20 first graders were killed in 2012.

In April 2013, as public attention faded, the families and organizations that had sprung up around gun issues changed their strategy. What started as a legislative campaign became an effort to build infrastructure for future fights.

The N.R.A. had spent decades doing exactly that. Long before Sandy Hook, before Columbine, it was working tirelessly to accumulate influence in Washington.

There was some organizing on the other side: The group now called the Brady Campaign to Prevent Gun Violence was instrumental in passing the 1993 Brady Law, which instituted federal background checks, and the 1994 Assault Weapons Ban, which prohibited some semiautomatic weapons. (The ban expired in 2004.) But Brady's influence was dwarfed by the N.R.A.'s single-issue voters, millions of dollars in political spending and preternatural ability to mobilize.

That power imbalance changed because of Sandy Hook.

DOUG MILLS/THE NEW YORK TIMES

President Barack Obama spoke in the Rose Garden in April 2013, after Congress failed to pass gun control bills.

The shooting itself instantly spawned new organizations. Within hours, Shannon Watts, a mother of five in Indiana, went looking for a gun-related equivalent to Mothers Against Drunk Driving and found none. So she created a Facebook page, which ballooned into Moms Demand Action.

Meanwhile, former Representative Gabrielle Giffords, who was almost killed by a gunman in 2011, was meeting with survivors in Newtown, helping prompt the creation of the group Sandy Hook Promise. Nationally, Ms. Giffords founded her own organization, Americans for Responsible Solutions, intensifying her earlier advocacy.

"It was that day we realized we had to do more," she said.

After April, the groups branched out. Po Murray, a Newtown resident, left Sandy Hook Promise to found the Newtown Action Alliance, which took an aggressive legislative approach focused on building support for an assault weapons ban, on the theory that less divisive policies would then follow more easily.

Sandy Hook Promise, led by Mr. Barden and Ms. Hockley, went in a different direction entirely, developing programs that would train students to recognize and report warning signs among classmates. (Those programs are now in place in 14,000 schools and have resulted in more than 3,000 tips, the group said. Some tips have led to arrests, including last month in Seymour, Conn.)

When the background checks bill failed, Ms. Watts briefly considered disbanding Moms Demand Action. Instead, she and the group decided to turn their focus to statehouses.

"Congress isn't where this work begins. It's more likely where it ends," Ms. Watts said. "And we would have to build the momentum."

Her group, which later joined with Mr. Bloomberg's Mayors Against Illegal Guns to form Everytown for Gun Safety, established a chapter in every state and began lobbying. Ms. Giffords's group worked on state legislation, too, but also mobilized gun owners, many of whom support stricter laws.

The cumulative result was an infrastructure that had previously existed only on the conservative side of gun policy. And in the wake of the Parkland shootings, those new groups made a huge difference in terms of organizing.

Part of the relationship was financial: When the Parkland students organized the March for Our Lives rally in Washington, Everytown helped fund companion marches around the country. But the bigger part was structural: The groups founded after Sandy Hook funneled what might otherwise have been raw grief and rage into organized advocacy.

This was true not only for the students, but for individuals nationwide who were compelled to action by Parkland just as Ms. Watts was by Newtown. Before the Parkland shooting, Moms Demand Action had 296 local groups. By last month, it had 735.

America still has some of the Western world's least restrictive gun laws. It has less than 5 percent of the world's population and about 40

KAYANA SZYMCZAK FOR THE NEW YORK TIMES

Shannon Watts, center, created the gun control group Moms Demand Action after the Sandy Hook shooting.

percent of its civilian gun ownership. Still, in terms of concrete legislative and electoral results, 2018 was a watershed.

States enacted more than three times as many gun control measures in 2018 as in 2017. In a major shift, gun control groups outspent the N.R.A. in the midterm elections. In October, Mr. Murphy identified eight close races where a Republican incumbent had an A rating from the N.R.A. and the Democratic challenger was running explicitly on gun restrictions; Democrats won all eight. Lucy McBath, who became a Moms Demand Action volunteer after her son, Jordan Davis, was shot, defeated another incumbent in a Republican district in Georgia.

The new Democratic House majority quickly introduced background check legislation, which became the first major gun control bill to clear either chamber of Congress in 25 years. Its prospects in the Senate are dim, but the Senate Judiciary Committee held a hearing on other restrictions last month — and Senator Lindsey Graham, a Republican and the committee chairman, announced that he was working on a bill to encourage red-flag laws.

Mr. Graham's office did not respond to interview requests, but he told the South Carolina newspaper The State: "I think most Americans believe that multiple murderers shouldn't have gun rights. Most Americans support background checks."

In a remark that would have been nearly unthinkable from a top Republican a few years ago, he added, "The Second Amendment's important to me, but it's not a suicide pact."

The N.R.A. vehemently denies its influence is waning, and there is no doubt it is still a powerful force. The group's spokeswoman, Jennifer Baker, argued that its support was "organic" and the other side's manufactured by wealthy donors, and that public opinion had not shifted.

"It's important not to confuse activity, paid phone calls, advertisements, increased activity on the gun control front there with actual support and votes," she said.

There is substantial data showing support for tougher gun laws, however. According to Gallup, 61 percent of Americans want stricter laws on gun sales, up from 43 percent in October 2011, the last time Gallup asked the question before Newtown.

And while there is still a sharp partisan divide in Congress, with most Republicans supporting the N.R.A. and most Democrats opposing it, there are new cracks. Mr. Graham isn't the only prominent Republican now on board with a red-flag bill; Senator Marco Rubio of Florida, who received an A+ rating from the N.R.A. when he was last up for re-election in 2016, also introduced one.

Six years after they stood in the Rose Garden feeling that they had failed, Ms. Hockley and Mr. Barden said they had come to believe that, maybe, it was better that it happened this way.

"I will admit that there is a small part of me that is glad it didn't pass in April 2013, because too many people could have said, 'That's it, job done, solved the problem,' " Ms. Hockley said. "That could have killed the movement."

A Gun Killed My Son. So Why Do I Want to Own One?

OPINION | BY GREGORY GIBSON | JUNE 1, 2019

While fighting for stricter gun laws, I was always told I didn't understand. Maybe now I do.

TO BE CLEAR, there was nothing I could've done to save him. It's just a fantasy that has been circling my brain in a holding pattern for decades — that somehow I could have intervened.

On the evening of Dec. 14, 1992, a student armed with a semiautomatic rifle fired into the guard shack at the entrance to Bard College at Simon's Rock in Great Barrington, Mass., seriously wounding the guard stationed there. Moments later a car pulled up to the guard shack and the killer shot point-blank into the car's side window. The driver died instantly and the car ran off the road. Someone heard the noise and rushed into the college library to report the accident. My son Galen, a sophomore at the college, rushed out the door to help. The shooter was waiting there, at the end of the sidewalk. Galen was hit twice; the chest shot was fatal. He staggered back into the library and died.

If my pistol and I had somehow been on the scene that night, no matter how highly trained we might've been, it's likely we'd have rushed out the door to see if we could render assistance in the reported auto accident. The killer would still have been there, and I'd have been shot instead of my son. Small comfort in that.

A FEW YEARS AGO, I was flying home to Massachusetts from the West Coast with a copy of The New Yorker to keep me company. As the cocktail cart approached, I came upon an article about Henry Worsley's doomed attempt to walk alone and unaided across the continent of Antarctica. He was a distant relative of the explorer Ernest Shackleton's comrade Frank Worsley, and he was obsessed with the idea of honoring those legendary explorers by repeating the journey. Exhaustion and

DAMON WINTER/THE NEW YORK TIMES

The author at a friend's home in the woods where he practices at a makeshift range.

illness brought him to a halt a mere 30 miles short of his goal. He was rescued and flown to Punta Arenas, Chile, but he died in the hospital of bacterial peritonitis.

Sitting in my comfy red-eye cocoon at 35,000 feet reading of his agonies on the ice, and of his even more agonizing decision to call for help so near the end of his walk, the poignancy of Worsley's story brought tears to my eyes. Then I thought of his wife and two children, and everything else he'd left behind, and my moist-eyed mood lifted. Why would anyone with so much to lose attempt such a stunt? Though the article never explicitly said as much, I could imagine only one explanation for Henry Worsley's crazy walk: He was using the continent of Antarctica and the extremity of the conditions he imposed upon himself to explore unknown regions of his psyche, his own interior portal to a vaster, universal interiority. I thought, *Ah! That's just what I'm doing!* Then I fell asleep.

Since that night I have had occasion to think of Henry Worsley.

My progress from survivor of gun violence to practitioner of defensive shooting proceeded in the same manner as Worsley's epic disaster.

Down at the pistol range, for example — a subterranean hall reminiscent of a bowling alley — firing my 9-millimeter Sig Sauer P320 at a man-sized paper silhouette during an advanced gun skills class. The air-treatment fans are running full blast, but about a dozen of us have been shooting for hours. I can taste the sweetness of vaporized lead in the back of my mouth.

Considering the role that guns have played in my life, such moments need explaining, and the Worsley trope is helpful in this regard. I could even imagine that my progress from traumatized survivor of gun violence to practitioner of tactical defensive shooting proceeded in the same manner as Worsley's epic disaster — step by step.

MY SON'S KILLER was a fellow student, a sophomore in the throes of a psychotic break. The administrators at Simon's Rock had seen the clearly labeled ammo package arrive in that morning's mail, and an anonymous call to a member of the staff warned that the killer had a gun and was planning to use it. But school shootings weren't seen as a national crisis in 1992; the dean and the administration hadn't been trained in active-shooter response because that body of knowledge didn't really exist back then. Those administrators were ill-equipped to prevent the shooting.

I was so furious at their failure that I sued the college. But the painstaking process of legal discovery served also as a trek through the sources of my grief. Eventually I realized that there was no redemption in revenge. I made peace with the college and became involved in the gun-violence-prevention movement, sharing my story with anyone who would listen. My relationship with guns at that time was uncomplicated. I'd hunted as a kid and I'd received basic firearms training when I joined the Navy in 1967, but like many people in the liberal circles in which I traveled, I believed that guns were stupid and awful and that there was something fundamentally wrong with people who liked to use them.

However, after 20 years of advocacy I was beginning to realize that something else was fundamentally wrong. I had always assumed that once people heard firsthand of the misery that a gun had caused, they'd be motivated to support laws that would prevent such tragedies from happening to anyone else. I kept believing this, and I kept telling my story, and Columbine, Virginia Tech and Aurora kept happening. On Friday in Virginia Beach, a city worker killed at least 12 people.

The real breaking point for me though, was, Dec. 14, 2012 — the 20th anniversary, to the day, of Galen's murder — 20 children and six adults were shot to death at Sandy Hook elementary school. An avalanche of heartbreaking stories poured forth and still America did nothing. This nothingness inspired me, in the howling void of my survivor's journey, to alter my course.

I'd been told repeatedly by gun owners — often from the back of whatever crowd I was addressing — that my arguments for gun control had little credibility because I knew nothing about guns or gun culture. Eventually I came to see some truth in that assertion. If there was a gun culture of Second Amendment zealots, there was also an opposing gun-control culture made up of people who knew little about guns except that guns were bad. People, in other words, like me.

Received wisdom had it that the two sides in the gun control "debate" would eventually hammer out a consensus resulting in "sensible" gun legislation that would "respect the Second Amendment" while making it harder for criminals and would-be mass murderers to get guns. But now it seemed that the implied dialectic was a sham, and that in fact the two sides were locked in a sterile opposition from which no consensus would ever emerge. America was in the midst of a culture war, not a debate. We were muddling our bloody way toward some new identity as a people, or perhaps our dissolution as a people, and no survivor's story would change that. For the first time since Galen's death, I saw the situation in a different light. That implied a step in the right direction, but I needed more information.

The long and the short of it is that I bought a gun.

I didn't just rush out and buy one; I took my time doing research. I had conversations with people at gun shows. I read gun magazines and spent hours on YouTube watching guys take guns apart and put them back together and blast the bejesus out of bottles full of colored water. I watched women shoot, and men and boys and girls shoot. And I have to admit, I did not care for these people and their guns. I found them aesthetically displeasing. But I stuck with it, and eventually it became somewhat more interesting to watch, for example, the YouTube video of the lady in Texas with the pink Beretta, or the guy shoulder bumping his AR so that it fired as if it were on full auto.

I signed up for the gun-safety course at my local gun club. In Massachusetts, this training was required by law to apply for a firearm license. Ninety-five dollars bought me a morning of instruction followed by a few minutes of wrapping my hands around cold steel (polymer, actually) and firing a real gun. It was an exciting moment for me and it was marked by an unusual occurrence.

Growing More Divided

Percent who say it is more important to protect the right of Americans to own guns than to control gun ownership, by party.

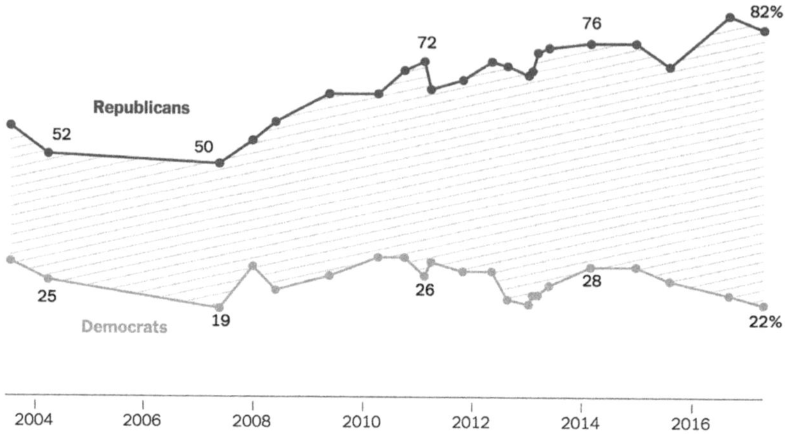

BY THE NEW YORK TIMES

Somehow, during the live-fire part of the course, an empty brass casing — probably from the pistol of the student next to me — found its way into the right pocket of the vest I'd worn to class. I didn't discover it until that afternoon, when I put my hand in the pocket and pulled out an expended .22 shell. I put it back in my pocket, and every time I stuck my hand in there I rolled the little brass cylinder around in my fingers. This produced an excitement from a place I could not identify.

I wore that vest to the police station a few days later. There, after surrendering my fingerprints, and producing my driver's license and the certificate from my gun course, I filled out the requisite paperwork and had an interview with a police officer regarding my application. I had been advised to answer "for all legal purposes" as my reason for obtaining a license, but she didn't ask me why I wanted to carry a gun. Instead, we bantered about local issues and characters and that was that. Some states are "shall issue" states, in which the local chief of police must issue a license to carry a firearm to any qualified applicant. Massachusetts is a "may issue" state, in which the chief has some discretion. This woman was his shrewd representative. A couple of weeks later I got a call from her. My license had come in.

When the weather warmed I visited my local gun shop and saw, in a glass case, a Ruger LC9s, a small 9-millimeter handgun that had gotten good reviews in the gun magazines. I'd already decided that I should begin my gun career with something modest, and this stubby little thing had an unassuming look to it. I took a calming breath and asked the guy behind the counter if I could handle the gun.

Soon I found myself engaged in a distinctly American rite of passage. I produced my driver's license and my recently acquired class A large-capacity license to carry firearms. The salesman gave me a form on which I entered my personal information and checked the "no" box next to each of a number of questions intended to ascertain my fitness to own a gun. Was I a drug addict? Had I ever been "adjudicated as a mental defective?" I could have been as disturbed as the kid who thought God was commanding him to kill my son, but if my criminal record was clean and if I kept a straight face, it's possible the purchase would have gone forward.

Pro-gun people are always talking about fixing the mental health system, but concrete proposals are in short supply. Meanwhile, the mental health community is fiercely protective of patient privacy, and these interests can run counter to the reporting necessary for any background check to be effective. The salesman took my paperwork into the back room, where he checked the six-digit PIN on my firearms license against the computerized state database and ran my information through the F.B.I.'s national instant criminal background check system. Fifteen minutes and a few hundred dollars later, I was an official gun owner.

Then I knew precisely the word for the feeling that shell casing gave me every time I felt for it in my vest pocket. The word was "transgressive" and the effect was steroidal. I was the father of a gun-murdered child and I had taken a gun course and obtained a gun license and purchased a gun. I wasn't supposed to be doing this, but I was doing it anyway.

Lax Laws, More Deaths

States with fewer gun restrictions had higher death rates from firearms. Most of the correlation is because of deaths from suicide, not homicide.

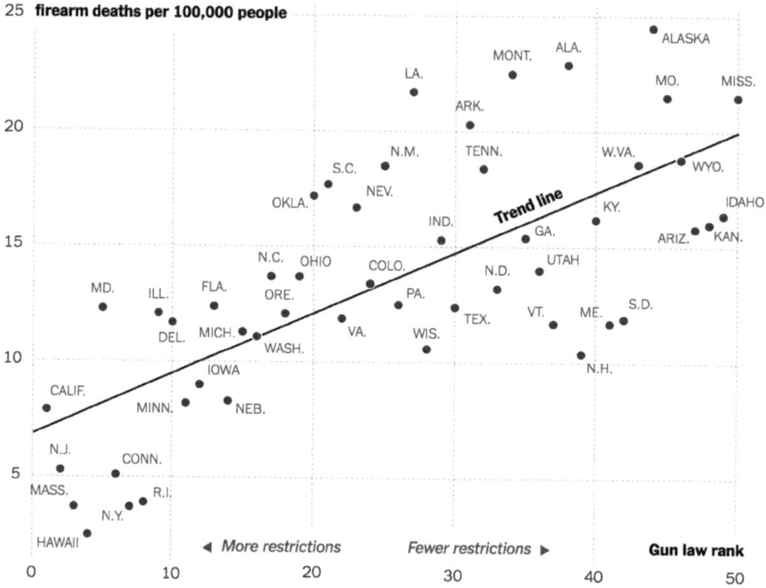

BY THE NEW YORK TIMES

Note: State gun law rank is a combination of the Giffords Law Center's Gun Law Scorecard rank and the Cato Institute's Freedom in the 50 States rank, a methodology based on an article from The Trace. Firearm mortality is from 2017.

One other realization accompanied the rush of power that surged through me. When you walk down the street knowing you are lethal, there can be no such thing as a "modest" gun. That was why the little Ruger remained so long in a drawer in my desk, rendered inoperative by a cable gun lock strung through its innards. Weeks passed before I was able to muster up the courage to try shooting the thing.

I have a friend who lives in the woods about half an hour from my house. Over the years he'd cleared a sort of firing range on which he practiced for the deer season, and when I explained my quest to him, he invited me to use it. We took a long walk through the field below his house to a pallet leaned up against a pile of rocks. A bullet-scarred squeeze clamp at the top of the pallet held a paper bull's-eye. Twenty paces and turn. The gun barked and jumped in my hand; the target escaped unscathed. Ten paces forward. Same result. Five more, down to 15 feet now, and a hit. Then a miss, then another hit.

After a few more rounds the muscles in my shoulders and neck began to ache. Standing sweating in the tall grass, mosquitoes humming around my ears, I looked at the gun. My hands were trembling. My loathing of guns had collided with my determination to master them. The impact was devastating.

Or was it? I recalled one of the more urbane YouTube gun gurus explaining that people have a natural aversion to holding things that explode. He illustrated his point by extending a lit firecracker at arm's length in front of his face, which was exactly how it felt each time I yanked on the trigger. He referred to the phenomenon as "reactive interference" and the cure for it was … I couldn't remember what the cure for it was. It probably involved signing up for his online gun tutorial. That night I found the business card of a firearms trainer that the salesman at the gun shop had given me. I called the man and we scheduled an introductory session at an indoor range not far from my house.

His name was Jerry. He was about my height, a little past middle age, with a neatly trimmed salt-and-pepper haircut and matching mustache. He told me he was a retired A.T.F. agent. He worked with a security firm and also trained civilians and professionals in everything from basic safety to advanced tactical shooting.

I told him my story about the death of my son, my advocacy work and my belief that this work could not be properly carried forward without learning about guns. He nodded solemnly, taking it all in, his eyebrows arching slightly at the "dead son" part. I noticed this reaction only because I was watching for it. Galen's death carries a peculiar power, potentially as deep as the grief that accompanies it. Over the years I've learned to deploy that power in a sort of grief-into-anger-into-action judo. I continue to believe that my attempts to turn dreck into gold give Galen, wherever he is, great satisfaction.

Jerry was an excellent teacher, full of stories, and somehow he imparted a calmness, a sense of control. He grinned and wiggled his index finger in front of my nose. "This is the only thing that will make the gun fire." I scheduled a second lesson, and as my schoolboy hunting days came back to me, I began to experience the Zen of the whole thing — the stance, the breathing, the focus, the squeeze. Then the acknowledgment from the pistol, which seemed almost jovial once I got used to it. An affirmative punch back at me. *There, now. Look what we've done!*

At the end of that lesson Jerry and I got to chatting. I asked him what he thought about the most recent mass shooting and he said, "It scares me."

"Really? Scared?"

"Every time these shootings happen, people run out and buy a gun, but not many of them will take the trouble to learn how to use it. Now when I go to the mall I get the creeps. All those guns in pockets and purses."

A FEW MONTHS AFTER MY LESSONS WITH JERRY, I was able to purchase a .40-caliber double action/single action pistol in a private sale from the family of a local man, recently deceased. My friend's woodland retreat rang with gunshots that fall.

Eventually I attained a modicum of proficiency with my two pistols. They no longer seemed alien or perverse. Shooting had become — dare I say it? — therapeutic. I was mastering the instrument of my suffering. Still, I could no more think of carrying a loaded gun on my person than I could imagine wearing a live chain saw.

Then Betsy DeVos came into my life.

Actually, Parkland came first. In February 2018, following the school shooting in Parkland, Fla., President Trump suggested arming teachers. "You give them a little bit of a bonus," he said. "So practically for free, you have now made the school into a hardened target." Then, that August, the Education Department and Secretary

DAMON WINTER/THE NEW YORK TIMES

Checking his results at the practice range.

of Education Betsy DeVos announced that they were considering allowing states to use a grant called the Student Support and Academic Enrichment program to finance the placement of guns in schools. Within a year, Florida and Texas passed bills allowing teachers, or increasing the number of teachers allowed, to carry guns in the classroom. The idea was out there, and it had taken root.

It took root in my imagination as well. Now, in that endless holding pattern of the re-enactment of Galen's murder, appears Secretary of Education Betsy DeVos, eyes wide behind those oversize eyeglasses, pulling a Baby Glock from her purse and going after the shooter. Or in her place, the librarian at the circulation desk, or the janitor. Or me. Again.

Except this time I have another reason for being there. I have a question: If we're going to give guns to teachers so that they can kill the killers who want to kill the students, how much training will the teachers need to be able to kill the killers without accidentally killing the students they're supposed to prevent the killers from killing?

I called Jerry.

So it was that I came to find myself engrossed in tactical defensive shooting, which proved to be at least as physically challenging and intellectually complex as mastering a flawless golf swing. My studies were also the occasion of a major surprise.

Jerry, the professional trainer of professional shooters, told me he thought arming teachers was a bad idea but that he'd take me and my project on. We had a relationship by this time and, full disclosure, I was paying him $50 an hour to get some sense of the kind and amount of training that an armed teacher would need to keep his or her students safe.

At first, under the pressure and urgency of my hypothetical teacher training, I had difficulty handling the guns. The Ruger was too small; I felt as if it might fly out of my hands. The .40 was difficult to operate with any speed or facility. I couldn't accustom myself to the first hard pull on the trigger. To make matters worse, I'm left handed. All the controls for both of the guns were positioned for right-handed shooters.

Toward the end of the second session, Jerry went inside his equipment bag and came out with a pistol that was a little smaller than my .40-caliber. "Try this," he said. "It's simpler to operate and it's ambidextrous." He put the gun in my hand and it fit in a way the other guns had not. It was a Sig Sauer P320, the gun that had recently been selected as the Army's official service pistol. I fired two or three rounds, then I didn't want to give it back. After the lesson ended, I could not stop thinking about how right that gun had felt.

That was a measure of how far I'd come. I took the Ruger and the .40 down to the gun shop and swapped them for a Sig Sauer P320 chambered in 9 millimeters — identical to the gun Jerry had lent me — and went home feeling a little loopy. Like falling in love for the first time, at least in the sense that I couldn't believe what was happening to me. I liked that gun. I *wanted* it.

My lessons proceeded apace, and after 20 hours of instruction and at least 30 more of practice on my own, I was comfortable enough to park my loaded gun in a hard plastic "appendix holster" inside my belt, beneath my shirt, pressing into my groin. I learned to extract it rapidly and safely, and shoot it more or less accurately, and reload and fire while turning, crouching, ducking in and out of concealment, never, ever, presenting a stationary target.

The only thing standing between me and mastery of tactical defensive shooting was me.

Throughout my training, with disconcerting irregularity, I would experience flashes of intense doubt, echoes of the first bad reaction that had come over me in my friend's field. I'd be overwhelmed by the realization that my experiment with guns was a childish, self-indulgent fantasy, disrespectful of the life Galen had lost and of all that my family had suffered.

MY PATIENT WIFE HAD SOME IDEA of what I was up to and found it distasteful in the extreme. My son, a burly, bearded contractor who looked like he should be the one with the Sig strapped on, thought I was nuts. A gun had killed his brother. Guns were stupid and awful and there was something fundamentally wrong with people who liked to use them. Of the three of them, my daughter seemed to have the most understanding of my Worsleyan venture. (I often wondered what his kids thought of what he'd done.) As with all my other advocacy projects, I was expending time and treasure in Galen's name. My family was proud of me for that, but it could not be denied that the time and treasure thus expended might otherwise have been spent on them.

What I was doing was wrong and it seemed wrongest when I had a gun in my hand, as happened one Saturday afternoon during one of Jerry's training classes. We were between drills when the feeling came upon me. I stuffed gleaming brass slugs into their magazines as if I were fingering prayer beads and tried to talk myself down. *I'm learning about guns so I can better understand the problem of gun violence in America, which will enable me to do a better job advocating against it.* (Whatever "it" was — a riddle that grew more complex the more I learned.) Three magazines loaded with 10 rounds apiece. Then on to our next exercise, the mirror drill, in which a full-length mirror is positioned between two shooters. One draws and the other reacts to what he sees in the mirror. Usually it would take three minutes to shoot through a ten-round magazine this way. That day it felt like an hour.

Being the sort of person I am, I combed the literature for information that would help me make sense of what I was feeling. Eventually, inevitably, I encountered the writings of Dave Grossman, a retired Army lieutenant colonel, pioneer researcher and scholar in the field of Killology (his designation, not mine, and a perfect example of his sometimes-tin ear). He is the author of "On Killing" and "On Combat" and is perhaps best known for an idea he discusses in those books that divides everyone into three distinct groups.

"If you have no capacity for violence then you are a healthy productive citizen: a sheep," he has written. "If you have a capacity for violence and no empathy for your fellow citizens, then you have defined an aggressive sociopath — a wolf. But what if you have a capacity for violence, and a deep love for your fellow citizens? Then you are a sheepdog, a warrior, someone who is walking the hero's path."

It seemed corny and unscientific to me. But if, as an actual sheepdog might, you see the world in black and white, its humorless piety, self-righteous rectitude and complete absence of subtlety would seem appealing.

In fairness, Colonel Grossman has done groundbreaking work delving into the psychology and physiology of killing. One of the starting points of his study is the observation that although we have little difficulty bombing whole nations into the Stone Age, we are hard-wired against killing one another face to face. Was that the source of my yips? I was, after all, training to shoot people at close range.

There was another aspect, laid out in exquisite detail by Colonel Grossman, to this business of up-close-and-personal killing. When one is under the extreme stress of having to do so, the forebrain stops giving orders and yields to the hypothalamus, the stress control center. Bladder and colon involuntarily empty, and the autonomic nervous system kicks in. The adrenal glands release potentially damaging levels of cortisol, adrenaline and other hormones. Blood pressure and respiration spike. Time seems to slow; nausea, auditory exclusion, tunnel vision and even temporary physical paralysis may ensue. Jerry never told us about any of that!

Post-Grossman I have a very different scenario of what takes place in my fantasy library in 1992. Professional trainers are largely in agreement that there's really no predicting how a person will react in a combat situation. No matter how diligently Betsy DeVos and I might have prepared, we'd be in the midst of a giant mess.

That was it for me. I airlifted myself out of there.

HAPPILY, I DIDN'T DIE OF PERITONITIS in a hospital in southern Chile. I wound up in a house of worship in northern New England. In the preface to "On Combat," Colonel Grossman wrote that he spends nearly 300 days a year traveling the country evangelizing the sheepdog mind-set. According to the Sheepdog Seminar website, he was coming soon to a church near Bangor, Me. I decided to go up there and hear what they had to say about the idea of people with guns keeping people safe from people with guns. One foot in front of the other.

About 150 of us were gathered at Calvary Chapel, a large modern building across the river from Bangor. Mostly men of middle age and beyond, with a smattering of women and teenagers. A few of us were carrying openly; many more had pistols concealed in baggy cargo pants or beneath untucked shirts. Jimmy Meeks, a minister and the director of the seminar, scooted back and forth in front of us, an agitated, white-haired penguin of a man, making Fox News jokes, church jokes about the uselessness of deacons, even a New England Patriots joke about deflation. Then he gave us the real news: Our country was in a season of violence, a holocaust of unprecedented dimension. Immigrants were pouring over the border like a freight train. Angry people were everywhere. "Our Heavenly Father's heart is broken over the violence," he announced, looking up toward the presumptive source of this information. "Our Heavenly Father intends to *respond* to the violence." He paused for a beat, then turned on the audience. "His response is ... you!"

I had some acquaintance with Mr. Meeks. He'd called me shortly after I submitted my online application for the seminar, to tell me that he'd looked me up and learned that there was a Gregory Gibson in my town who'd lost a son in a school shooting. (Being good sheepdogs, I supposed, they researched every seminar applicant who hadn't been vetted by the sponsoring church.) Was I that Gregory Gibson? I said that I was, and that he could call me Greg, since Gregory was merely my internet moniker, to distinguish me from the Major League Baseball umpire named Greg Gibson. That elicited a cackle and then a moan, as he told me how sorry he was for the unimaginable loss I had suffered. He was calling, he said, because he was concerned that I hadn't understood the nature of the Sheepdog Seminar. It was primarily about how church people could keep their churches safe, though the information would be useful to anyone. He was worried that I might be traumatized by some of the material in the presentation.

Perhaps it was the twang in his speech, so fresh to my ear. The way he'd said, "It breaks my heart" gave me the feeling that if I had burst into tears at that moment, he would have wept with me. He began telling me his story. He was 61 years old, a retired cop and a preacher, Southern Baptist. There were issues with his family back home in Texas. He wanted so much to be there with them but he couldn't stop traveling. He was driven by love. His voice wobbled. He took a breath and told me, "I'm a very emotional guy." Despite my reservations about sheepdogs and preachers, I found myself falling for the Rev. Jimmy Meeks, calling me out of the blue the way he had, to be sure I wouldn't be traumatized, to tell me how sorry he was for my loss and to share with me a glimpse of his own travails.

On either side of the stage at the front of Calvary Chapel was a big screen. "Matthew 10:17" appeared on both of them. Mr. Meeks read it, loud and slow, to be sure he had our attention. Then, for those of us — probably a minority — who hadn't memorized chapter and verse, he flashed the text beneath it. "Be on GUARD against men; they will flog you IN their synagogues." This was followed by a list of 50 headlines, also projected onto the screens, highlighting some of the "811 VIOLENT DEATHS" that had occurred on faith-based property since 1999.

Over the course of the two-day seminar, two case studies were presented and analyzed in detail by people who had shot and killed, or participated in the shooting and killing of, armed persons attempting mass murders. There were important things to be learned from these brave presenters, a great many things, ordered, elucidated and drilled into us by Jimmy Meeks — urging, weeping, scorning, confessing, praying. He called me out at one point, actually called my name and asked me to stand as he told my story, his voice quavering again. Poor planning. No training. Officials in denial. People approached me after that, shyly offering their condolences.

Yes, there would be guns, but the people carrying them would be the *right* people.

In the evening, at the end of the first day, we recited the Pledge of Allegiance, hands over hearts, sang the national anthem and "America the Beautiful" with lyrics to all the verses projected onto those same screens that had listed the grisly church crimes. Then we prayed, as Jimmy admonished us, "with your eyes open and your heads up!" and I thought how sweet it would be, if Christ had ever come into my life, to be dwelling in the bosom of the church with these strange, earnest people. How comforting it would be to know what to do. To have a plan. Yes, there would be guns, but the people carrying them would be the *right* people, carefully selected, thoroughly trained. In that moment of communal prayer, I had no doubt that I could trust these people with guns.

Colonel Grossman joined us on the second day of the seminar. He was fit and wiry, constantly in motion, delivering his pitch, very much the military man, punctuating his utterances with "Do you understand?" — as much a command as a question. He had a growly way of speaking and a rhythmic vocal tic, a sort of grunt or "umph" that reminded me of a sheepdog's affirmative "Ruff!" It pleased me to imagine that after decades of researching, formulating and evangelizing the sheepdog mind-set, Dave Grossman had become one.

He gave a brief pitch for his many books that pertained to the matter at hand. "Why Mommy Carries a Gun" is one title that stuck in my mind. Then he told us what he had learned from training soldiers, from desensitizing them to their natural aversion to killing up close. The terrible news he brought us on this day was that our national video game addiction was creating a generation of killers.

Guns had always been present in our society, he said, but there had been no multiple homicides by a juvenile in schools until the 1970s. Guns didn't change; *we* changed. He talked the pioneering work of Dr. James McGee, a co-author of the groundbreaking "Classroom Avenger" study on school shooters. According to Dr. McGee, the one thing these young killers had in common was that they were loners, and, in Colonel Grossman's telling, immersed themselves in "sicko movies and video games." He described video games as a form of "pathological play" that rewarded the player for causing death. Colonel Grossman's take on the research got more dire: Violent visual imagery actually changed the brains of players. Video games were digital crack. The media were taking no responsibility for the content they put out there. The mental health of an entire generation was a stake.

It was a chilling performance. I thought of my 7-year-old grandson, hunched over his tablet, keeping the world safe from zombies.

After it was over, Jimmy Meeks took me up to meet Colonel Grossman. I told him I'd read and been impressed by his work. He thanked me and inscribed a copy of one of his books for me. The book was about video games. It was called "Assassination Generation."

AS IT HAPPENED, I HAD BUSINESS in Washington the week after I attended the

Sheepdog Seminar. And as it also happened, I knew Dr. James McGee, the expert to whom Colonel Grossman had alluded. I'd met him 20 years before at a seminar on school safety and threat assessment, and we'd become friends. I decided to visit him at his home outside Baltimore.

He's a twinkly eyed, avuncular guy, with a record of achievement that belies his genial affect, including service as a recon Marine — their inside joke is that they're the ones who show up when the SEALS dial 911. He is a trained hostage negotiator, special consultant to the F.B.I.'s critical incident response group, retired director of psychology at Sheppard Pratt Hospital in Baltimore and, charmingly, team psychologist for the Baltimore Orioles in the 1980s, including the year they won the World Series, with a big, clunky World Series ring to show for it.

According to Dr. McGee, giving guns to teachers doesn't even merit serious discussion except in terms of bad outcomes. Cops become cops because they want to be cops. Teachers, by and large, do not want to become killers. But even in the hands of professionals, there was no guarantee of success. He told me that the accuracy rate of police officers in real gunfights is nothing to be confident about and that the accuracy rate in a classroom would be even worse because of the possibility of collateral damage, whereas the shooter would have no such concern. "Assumption of accuracy is not a deterrent for suicidal people," he said. In Dr. McGee's learned opinion, resources would be better spent on hardening targets (which, essentially, was the point of the two days I'd spent at the Sheepdog Seminar) and on threat assessment.

We sat in his living room sipping tea. A fluffy little dog and an exotic bobtail cat, both rescue animals, mooched around looking for treats or pats. Birds sang nesting songs outside and a spring breeze wafted through the room. We talked about Menninger's triad (wish to die + wish to kill + wish to be killed), the duty of clinicians to warn of serious threats from patients, the work of Dr. David Phillips on cluster suicides, the media's role in the increasing sophistication of classroom shootings and similarly grotesque topics. Much as the Rev. Jimmy Meeks had quoted scripture and Colonel Grossman had repeated "Do you understand?," Dr. James McGee ended many of his utterances with "You can look it up."

We went downstairs and admired his basement full of S-gauge and O-gauge model trains, laid out in switch yards and freight depots and small-town stations, tidy worlds in perfect miniature. We walked back to my car and talked about the road trip we'd take together some day, while we still could, and then I headed south.

That was when the trouble started.

AS I DROVE, I THOUGHT ABOUT THE GROUND I'D COVERED since deciding to become a gun owner. I'd assumed that my experiences along the way would lead to a deeper understanding of gun violence in America and that I would emerge at the end of my journey a more effective advocate of gun safety. I was therefore surprised to discover that in a certain sense, I hadn't made any progress at all. I'd started out believing that giving guns to teachers was a bad idea, and here I was, driving down Interstate 95 thinking that there were things we could do to make schools safer but that giving guns to teachers was not one of them. I'd stumbled around in a circle and come right back to where I'd started.

Now, though, the wrongness of arming teachers was more than a mere notion. I'd tested my ideas with help from Jerry, Colonel Grossman, Mr. Meeks, Dr. McGee, Secretary DeVos and President Trump. (I'd been enraged by his "practically for free" statement about school safety. Only later did I realize how that rage had propelled me.) I'd also tested my theories with all the people I'd spoken with at gun shows, the gun shop clerks and habitués, and my fellow trainees — as good, bad and ugly as any random lot of folks, except that many of them saw no connection between gun violence and their own interest in guns.

All of them would agree that what happened Friday in Virginia Beach was a revolting tragedy, but what did that have to do with what he was doing? For some, this decoupling of guns and gun violence was accompanied by a link between fear and demand. If the world was a threatening place and gun grabbers were going to make it impossible to get the guns we needed to protect ourselves, didn't it make sense to get more while we still could? I know. It's a minuscule sample size, but that's not the point. There were consequences to all the interacting and information-gathering I'd been doing. What if the beliefs I'd encountered weren't gun-nut pathology but simply a worldview oriented 180 degrees from the one to which I was accustomed?

I considered the power of the sad story I'd shared for all those years with hungry journalists who gobbled my suffering and pushed out content, and the pink-faced politicians brought to the verge of tears by the recitation of my sorrows, who then went out and voted against me. I considered my friend with the house in the woods. The first time I used his shooting range I asked him — this guy who routinely kills, butchers and eats the animals who share the forest with him — whether he wanted to take a few shots with my Ruger. He looked at the pistol and made a face. "No, thanks," he said. "I'm good."

I considered the fact that in hopes of becoming a more effective advocate, I had ceased advocating altogether. Now I was simply bearing witness. Where I'd expected fewer certainties, I discovered many more, and they all came in diametrically opposed pairs. My wife and children and I had lost our beloved Galen in the most hideous, random, wasteful way, and yet I could not see the world as a threatening place. I was a perfect sheep, except for the loaded gun nestled in my crotch.

Blacks and whites of the gun control debate smeared into gray. I'd gotten pretty comfortable with shooting, but even better (I thought!) at living in a perpetual state of cognitive dissonance, as if I had consumed America's gun problem and now embodied it. But when it came to actual people and realistic approaches to the problem of gun violence, black and white were still worlds apart. Focusing on legislation as a means of reducing gun deaths felt to me like a project for white people — detached from the ways in which systemic racism and economic exclusion drove gun violence. I'd spent a fair amount of time doing advocacy work in urban neighborhoods. From talking with people there, I knew that when your main concern is raising money to bury your 14-year old son or getting the police to investigate the murder of your husband, crafting sensible gun legislation can seem like an afterthought.

I drove on, and the opposing terms in my internalized gun-violence "debate" began canceling one another out. Instead of synthesis or consensus, I was left with nothing. What was the point of advocacy, anyway? It hadn't worked because it didn't work. Nothing I could do would rid the world of sociopaths and criminals. By the time I reached my hotel in Washington, I was a wreck. Somehow, inadvertently, I'd succeeded in breaking myself down completely, much as Navy boot camp broke civilian recruits down before building us back up as sailors. I must confess that I experienced a few difficult weeks after my visit with Jim McGee. I'm just beginning to rebuild.

I THINK I'LL KEEP SHOOTING. I enjoy it, and I want to see whether I can become more efficient and more accurate. And I'll resume my advocacy work, but I'm going to go about it differently. As with school safety, there are things we can do to reduce gun deaths. Some of them will require education and cultural change, some can be addressed through legislation. Would every Second Amendment zealot have to lose a child in a preventable gun death to understand the sense in this?

It's a terrible thought, and one I don't need to think. I'm thinking instead of Jimmy Meeks's God telling his flock that they were the answer. More than 125,000 people a year are killed or wounded by guns in America, and each of them is surrounded by friends, relatives and loved ones — a million people a year whose lives will never be the same because of that experience.

According to one poll, 58 percent of American adults have said that they or someone they care for has experienced gun violence. Those are the people I want to talk with now. That's my church.

GREGORY GIBSON is the author of "Gone Boy: A Father's Search for the Truth in His Son's Murder." An interview he conducted with the man who killed his son is available at goneboy.com.

CHAPTER 3

Factors Affecting Rights

The debate over gun rights involves many factors. Some of these have to do with individuals who have had their right to own guns removed, including those deemed not mentally fit to own guns and those who have been convicted of felonies. Some, however, argue that focusing on mental illness is counterproductive.

Some With Histories of Mental Illness Petition to Get Their Gun Rights Back

BY MICHAEL LUO | JULY 2, 2011

PULASKI, VA. — In May 2009, Sam French hit bottom, once again. A relative found him face down in his carport "talking gibberish," according to court records. He later told medical personnel that he had been conversing with a bear in his backyard and hearing voices. His family figured he had gone off his medication for bipolar disorder, and a judge ordered him involuntarily committed — the fourth time in five years he had been hospitalized by court order.

When Mr. French's daughter discovered that her father's commitment meant it was illegal for him to have firearms, she and her husband removed his cache of 15 long guns and three handguns, and kept them after Mr. French was released in January 2010 on a new regime of mood-stabilizing drugs.

Ten months later, he appeared in General District Court — the body that handles small claims and traffic infractions — to ask a judge to restore his gun rights. After a brief hearing, in which Mr. French's lengthy history of relapses never came up, he walked out with an order reinstating his right to possess firearms.

The next day, Mr. French retrieved his guns.

"The judge didn't ask me a whole lot," said Mr. French, now 62. "He just said: 'How was I doing? Was I taking my medicine like I was supposed to?' I said, 'Yes, sir.' "

Across the country, states are increasingly allowing people like Mr. French, who lost their firearm rights because of mental illness, to petition to have them restored.

A handful of states have had such restoration laws on their books for some time, but with little notice, more than 20 states have passed similar measures since 2008. This surge can be traced to a law passed by Congress after the 2007 massacre at Virginia Tech that was actually meant to make it harder for people with mental illness to get guns.

As a condition of its support for the measure, the National Rifle Association extracted a concession: the inclusion of a mechanism for restoring firearms rights to those who lost them for mental health reasons.

The intent of these state laws is to enable people to regain the right to buy and possess firearms if it is determined that they are not a threat to public safety. But an examination of restoration procedures across the country, along with dozens of cases, shows that the process for making that determination is governed in many places by vague standards and few specific requirements.

States have mostly entrusted these decisions to judges, who are often ill-equipped to conduct investigations from the bench. Many seemed willing to simply give petitioners the benefit of the doubt. The results often seem haphazard.

At least a few hundred people with histories of mental health issues already get their gun rights back each year. The number promises to grow, since most of the new state laws are just beginning to take effect. And in November, the Department of Veterans Affairs responded to the federal legislation by establishing a rights restoration process for more than 100,000 veterans who have lost their gun privileges after being designated mentally incompetent by the agency.

The issue goes to the heart of the nation's complicated relationship with guns, testing the delicate balance between the need to safeguard the public and the dictates of what the Supreme Court has proclaimed to be a fundamental constitutional right.

Mike Fleenor, the commonwealth's attorney here in Pulaski County, whose office opposed restoring Mr. French's rights, worries that the balance is being thrown off by weak standards.

"I think that reasonable people can disagree about issues of the Second Amendment and gun control and things like that, but I don't believe that any reasonable person believes that a mentally ill person needs a firearm," Mr. Fleenor said. "The public has a right to be safe in their community."

In case after case examined by The New York Times, judges made decisions without important information about an applicant's mental health.

Larry Lamb, a Vietnam veteran from San Diego who has suffered from depression and post-traumatic stress disorder, lost his gun rights and his cache of weapons in 2006 when he was involuntarily hospitalized after his dog's death left him suicidal. A psychiatrist who examined Mr. Lamb wrote that he "is extremely paranoid with a full-blown P.T.S.D., believing that he is still at war in the active military and he is a personal bodyguard of the president and many senators."

In early 2008, a Superior Court judge in San Diego granted Mr. Lamb's petition to have his firearms rights restored, after his psychologist testified that he was not dangerous. But the judge, without access to Mr. Lamb's full medical history, was unaware of a crucial fact: the local Veterans Affairs hospital had placed a "red flag" on Mr. Lamb, barring him from the hospital grounds because he was perceived to be a threat to personnel there.

The spread of these restoration laws is especially striking against the backdrop of the shooting of Representative Gabrielle Giffords of

Arizona and others in Tucson early this year by a suspect who has been declared mentally incompetent to stand trial — a case that spotlighted anew the link between mental illness and violence.

Supporters of gun rights and mental health advocates point out that a vast majority of people with mental illness are not violent. At the same time, though, a variety of studies have found that people with serious mental illness are more prone to violence than the general population.

The difficulty of assessing risk emerges in places like Los Angeles, where the Superior Court conducts a relatively thorough review of firearms rights requests. The Times found multiple instances over the last decade in which people who won back their gun rights went on to be charged with or convicted of violent or gun-related crimes, including spousal battery, negligent discharge of a firearm or assault with a firearm.

Then there are the nightmare cases — like that of Ryan Anthony, 35, a former Emmy Award-winning animator at Disney who was involuntarily hospitalized in mid-2001 after losing his job and separating from his wife. Mr. Anthony filed a petition to get back his gun rights in early 2002, telling a court-appointed psychiatrist that he wanted to go skeet shooting.

A few weeks after the court granted his petition, Mr. Anthony bought a Remington 870 12-gauge shotgun, holed up in a Holiday Inn in Burbank, Calif., and committed suicide.

AN N.R.A. VICTORY

The galvanizing revelation for gun-control advocates after the Virginia Tech massacre, the worst mass shooting in American history, was that the gunman, Seung-Hui Cho, should never have been able to buy the guns he used in the rampage.

Two years earlier, a special justice declared Mr. Cho “an imminent danger to himself as a result of mental illness” and ordered him to outpatient treatment.

Under federal law, anyone involuntarily committed or adjudicated a "mental defective" is barred from buying or possessing firearms. But the prohibition is often toothless because many states do not share their mental health records with the F.B.I.'s National Instant Criminal Background Check System.

Mr. Cho's case offered Representative Carolyn McCarthy, Democrat of New York, a chance to advance a stalled bill that she had sponsored several years earlier to improve reporting by states to the F.B.I. database.

Ms. McCarthy's political career and commitment to gun control was born out of tragedy. In 1993, a deranged gunman opened fire on a commuter train on Long Island, killing six people, including her husband, and gravely injuring her son. After more than a decade working on the issue in Congress, however, she had little to show for it.

Ms. McCarthy said she was wiser after years of setbacks. "I don't believe in introducing legislation that won't go anywhere," she said.

She joined forces with Representative John D. Dingell, a Michigan Democrat and former N.R.A. board member, who acted as a liaison with the gun lobby. The N.R.A. had long been interested in gun-rights restoration. It also wanted to help tens of thousands of veterans who lost their rights after being designated mentally incompetent and unable to handle their finances by the Department of Veterans Affairs.

"We don't want to treat our soldiers as potential criminals because they're struggling with the aftermath of dealing with their service," said Chris Cox, the association's chief lobbyist.

The gun lobby secured a broad provision in the legislation. The new law made money available to states to help improve their record sharing, but the provision pushed by the N.R.A. made it a prerequisite for states to establish a "relief from disability" program for people with histories of mental health issues to apply for the restoration of gun rights. The Veterans Affairs Department and other federal agencies were required to do the same.

Gun-control groups attacked the provisions. "You make one bad judgment, and you could have another Virginia Tech on your hands," Kristen Rand, legislative director for the Violence Policy Center, said in an interview.

But the most prominent gun-control organization, the Brady Campaign to Prevent Gun Violence, ultimately supported the bill. "She felt if she didn't do this, it wasn't going to proceed," Paul Helmke, the group's president, said of Ms. McCarthy. "An imperfect bill is better than no bill."

Ms. McCarthy said her background as a nurse made her amenable to restoring someone's rights, "if they could prove they are no longer mentally ill."

After the bill became law in 2008, the N.R.A. began lobbying state lawmakers to keep requirements for petitioners to a minimum.

In Idaho, for example, a committee of law enforcement and mental health officials proposed requiring courts to make findings by "clear and convincing" evidence and mandating that petitioners have a recent mental health evaluation. But without the N.R.A.'s imprimatur, the legislation went nowhere.

Instead, a Republican state representative, Raúl R. Labrador, who is now a congressman, worked with the N.R.A. to draft a bill, passed last year, that dropped the requirement for a mental health evaluation and lowered the standard of proof to a "preponderance of evidence."

A few states have set stricter standards. In New York, decisions are made by mental health officials, and applicants must submit a long list of documents, including five years' worth of medical records and records of psychiatric and substance abuse treatment going back 20 years. State officials can also require applicants to undergo clinical evaluations and risk assessments.

So far, there has been only a trickle of petitions in states with new restoration laws. The statutes are not yet well known, and federal authorities have yet to certify many of the state programs, making them fully operational under federal law.

But the demand will almost certainly grow, given the experience of states with longer-standing restoration statutes. In California, for instance, judges restored gun rights to 180 people in 2010. At the federal level, the Veterans Affairs Department has already received more than 100 applications, of which 12 were processed and one was granted.

As for the original aim of Ms. McCarthy's legislation, the reporting of mental health records by states to the F.B.I. database remains woeful. The reasons vary, including privacy laws, technological challenges and inattention from state officials.

But one significant hurdle has been that only a handful of states have received the federal money to improve their reporting capabilities. Officials with the Bureau of Justice Statistics indicated that while 22 states applied for grants in 2009 and 2010, only nine have gotten financing. Most of those that did not receive grants were rejected because they did not have certified restoration programs in place.

ONE STATE'S EXPERIENCE

Lawmakers in Virginia, the scene of Mr. Cho's rampage, were among the first to respond to the federal legislation by amending the state's existing restoration statute to reflect the new law. To restore firearms rights, judges must find that the petitioner "will not likely act in a manner dangerous to public safety" and that "the granting of the relief would not be contrary to the public interest." There are few specific standards or guidelines beyond that.

In 2010, judges in Virginia considered roughly 40 restoration applications and granted firearms rights under state law to 25 people — 14 who had been involuntarily committed, and 11 who had been the subjects of temporary detention orders and were voluntarily admitted for mental health treatment, according to figures from the Virginia Supreme Court and the State Police. In 2009, the courts restored rights to 21 people.

There is no central repository for cases heard around Virginia, but to get a picture of how the process works in one state, The Times obtained dozens of petitions and judges' orders, mainly from 2009 and 2010, along with supporting documentation, and interviewed petitioners, lawyers and judges. The hearings were often relatively brief, sometimes perfunctory, and judges had wide latitude in handling the petitions.

Teresa Hall, who had moved to Idaho, said she simply wrote a letter to Hampton General District Court explaining that her commitment several years earlier occurred when she was experiencing marital difficulties. To her shock, she got a judge's order granting her petition several days later in the mail.

"I was surprised it was that easy," Ms. Hall said.

Some judges insisted on seeing a doctor's note, but others did not.

In a typical case, Joshua St. Clair, who served in Iraq with the National Guard, got his gun rights back last year. About six months earlier, Mr. St. Clair, now 22, had heard a rattling at his gate. He said he "kind of blacked out" and the next thing he knew, he was pointing his M-4 assault rifle at his friend's chest. That led to a temporary detention order, treatment for post-traumatic stress disorder and loss of his firearms rights.

He took a note from his psychiatrist to his restoration hearing, which he said "lasted maybe about five minutes," but he said the judge did not even ask to see it. The judge asked Mr. St. Clair's father a few questions and asked Mr. St. Clair himself whether he thought he should have his rights restored. He said, "Of course."

Often the doctors' recommendations came from general practitioners, not mental health professionals. The notes tended to be short, often just a few sentences.

In many cases, the hospitalizations occurred just a few months, or even weeks, earlier.

Bobby Bullion, 37, got his gun rights back about four months after he left a note for his wife and son that indicated he was considering suicide — his wife had told him she was divorcing him — and the police found him in his car with two loaded weapons. Mr. Bullion presented the judge with a letter from his psychiatrist endorsing the restoration.

DON PETERSEN FOR THE NEW YORK TIMES

Mr. Bullion, showing how he carries a gun in his truck, got his rights back with a doctor's endorsement.

Oran Greenway, 68, had his rights restored in August, just two months after he was involuntarily committed. The judge's restoration shocked Mr. Greenway's relatives, who said they had been worried for years about his mental stability. In an interview, he said he started taking Lexapro for depression several years ago. In 2005, he slammed a large branch on a neighbor's head during an argument, resulting in a conviction for assault and battery.

"Knowing what I know about Oran, I wouldn't let Oran have a gun," said Elizabeth Dequino, a cousin who lives up the road.

Even when a court-ordered commitment occurred years ago, the wisdom of restoring certain petitioners' firearms rights was open to question. David Neal Moon, 63, was involuntarily committed in 1995 after his struggles with schizoaffective bipolar disorder got so bad that he had threatened to commit suicide and was walking in circles around his house with a MAK-90 assault rifle, as if on guard duty, according to medical and court records and an interview with Cynthia Allison, who is now his ex-wife.

A psychiatrist's report described him threatening to "bash in the face of his wife" and ranting about getting his guns so he could "shoot everybody." It also mentions a violent hair-pulling episode with his wife.

He had not been committed since, but he had continued to struggle with his illness and was bad about taking his medication, Ms. Allison said.

In an interview, Mr. Moon insisted he took his medication and was not mentally ill. Yet he alluded to his phone being tapped by the State Police and "by maybe the Pentagon."

His firearms hearing in early 2009 in Amherst General District Court, where Mr. Moon showed up in military camouflage, lasted "about eight minutes," said Mr. Moon's lawyer, Gregory Smith, adding that he did not recall presenting any recent medical evaluation.

Just over a month later, another judge granted Ms. Allison a protective order against her husband. The pair had split up, and Mr. Moon had been making veiled threats by phone and telling his children about demons in the walls, according to her court affidavit.

"The judge just sat there and listened to him talk," Ms. Allison said. "I didn't even say anything. If you listened to him talk, you could tell he's as crazy as a bedbug."

Among those whose applications were denied, many were turned down for technical reasons, like filing in the wrong jurisdiction or failing to show up for a hearing.

In others cases — like one last year in Lynchburg in which the petitioner, Undreas Smith, submitted a letter explaining he had been struggling with recent deaths in his family — the judge ruled against the petitioner because he failed to provide documentation from a mental health provider.

In the case of James Tuckson Jr. of Harrisonburg, who was involuntarily committed in 2006 and applied in October to get back his gun rights, prosecutors said his multiple arrests probably played a significant role in the judge's decision to deny Mr. Tuckson's petition.

Presented with The Times's findings, Richard Bonnie, the chairman of the Virginia Commission on Mental Health Law Reform, which was formed after the Virginia Tech shootings, expressed concerns about the restoration process, particularly the vagueness of the statute. Mr. Bonnie said the panel would begin collecting information on the petitions on a monthly basis to better evaluate how they were being handled.

"There is an ambiguity in the statute that we need to look at," he said.

'A HOLE IN THE PROCESS'

When Sam French, the man with bipolar disorder whose daughter removed his guns, appeared late last year in Pulaski General District Court, he presented his recent medical records. Progress notes over several months showed that his bipolar disorder and substance abuse were in "remission."

Nevertheless, Bobby Lilly, an assistant commonwealth's attorney, opposed the petition, partly because Mr. French's latest update indicated he had expressed interest in lowering the dosage of his medication. Mr. French's two most recent hospitalizations had come after he went off his medication.

Mr. Lilly was also worried because it had been less than a year since his release. "We didn't have a demonstrated track record of being able to comply with whatever the mental health provider's directives were," Mr. Lilly said.

In fact, a few months later, in March, a judge at the circuit level — the higher court in Virginia — denied Mr. French's application for a concealed weapons permit because a five-year wait after a psychiatric commitment is required for such a permit.

But there is no waiting period for the restoration of basic gun rights.

Mr. French's case fell to Judge Royce Glenwood Lookabill, a genial presence on the bench since 2006. Judge Lookabill said he quizzed Mr. French about whether he had had any other episodes and whether he was taking his prescribed drugs.

DON PETERSEN FOR THE NEW YORK TIMES

David Neal Moon outside his home in Amherst County, Va., in April.

"I was satisfied that he wasn't a danger — again, subject to him taking his medication," Judge Lookabill said in an interview.

The judge acknowledged, however, that he might have made a different decision had he been aware of Mr. French's previous commitments, including one that came after he was arrested for public drunkenness and later allegedly assaulted two police officers. (The assault charges were dropped.) No one had checked a state database for his commitment history.

"It's a hole in the process," said Mr. Lilly, who added that his office had only limited access to such information.

Judge Lookabill suggested that the process belonged in a higher court and should be made more adversarial. "I would feel a lot more comfortable," he said, "if there were more safeguards."

AN INCREASED RISK

Most people with mental health issues, of course, will never be violent.

But there is widespread consensus among scientists that the increased risk of violence among those with a serious mental illness — schizophrenia, major depression or bipolar disorder — is statistically significant. That risk rises when substance abuse, which is more prevalent among people with mental illness, is also present.

One frequently cited study, led by Jeffrey W. Swanson, an expert on mental health and violence who is now at Duke University, showed that 33 percent of people with a serious mental illness reported past violent behavior, compared with 15 percent of people without a major mental disorder. Violent behavior was defined as including acts ranging from taking part in more than one fistfight as an adult to using a weapon in a fight. The rate for those with substance abuse issues but without a serious mental illness was 55 percent. The highest rate, 64 percent, was exhibited by people with major mental disorders and substance abuse issues.

Other studies have concluded that additional factors significantly increase the risk of violence among people with mental illness, including exposure to violence and being a victim of violence.

But taking these data and applying them to individuals is profoundly difficult.

Scientists have concluded that it is most accurate to augment clinical judgments with an "actuarial" approach, in which variables like psychiatric diagnosis, history of violence and anger control are plugged into a risk assessment model. The models categorize people into higher and lower risk groups. But many clinicians are unfamiliar with the technique. Indeed, none of the doctors who wrote letters on behalf of their patients in cases The Times reviewed appeared to utilize the approach.

Doctors' declarations clearly influenced judges. But most wrote their letters at the request of their patients, which Randy Otto, a former president of the American Board of Forensic Psychology and an associate professor at the University of South Florida, said can be problematic.

"They're more subject to pressure from their patients to offer opinions that will help the patients get what they want," Dr. Otto said.

He said many doctors, particularly those not in the mental health field, are probably not steeped in the most important clues to future violence. Even psychologists and psychiatrists, relying on their clinical judgment alone, are extremely unreliable in predicting violence, studies have shown.

"Unstructured clinical judgments, just judgments of mental health professionals about how risky someone is," Dr. Otto said, "are probably the least reliable and the least accurate."

WEIGHING THE THREATS

The difficulties of predicting violence are particularly striking in Los Angeles County, where the Superior Court has a relatively rigorous process for determining whether to restore gun rights.

In California, anyone placed on a 72-hour or 14-day psychiatric hold and determined to be a danger to themselves or others loses gun rights for five years. But upon discharge, the person can apply to have these prohibitions lifted. Applicants in Los Angeles County are required to provide records from all involuntary hospitalizations, which are checked against a list provided by the State Department of Justice. They must also be examined by a court-appointed psychiatrist, who can call friends or relatives to gather more information.

Under the statute, the burden is on the district attorney to establish that the petitioner "would not be likely to use firearms in a safe and lawful manner."

Over all, 1,579 petitions have been filed in Los Angeles Superior Court since 2000. More than 1,000 were dismissed, usually because applicants did not furnish the required documentation or failed to show up. Of those who actually got hearings, 381 won their cases.

"Dealing with somebody who suffers from severe mental illness and mixing that with firearms, you really have to cross the t's and dot the i's," said Richard J. Vagnozzi, a deputy district attorney who handles these cases. Mr. Vagnozzi said the process "isn't perfect, but we do the best we can with the available data and what we're allowed to do."

Even with the vigorous checks, there are people like Afshin Poordavoud, who lost his gun rights in June 2000. During a heated argument with his brother, Mr. Poordavoud threatened to shoot himself. His brother called the police, and Mr. Poordavoud was hospitalized briefly, according to court records.

Several months later, Mr. Poordavoud petitioned to have his firearms rights restored and to have the police return his shotgun and 9-millimeter semiautomatic handgun. A court-appointed psychiatrist recommended that the decision be put off for three months and that Mr. Poordavoud get a full psychiatric evaluation and treatment, pointing out that the hospital had found him to be "likely depressed and minimizing his level of depression and suicidal risk."

Mr. Poordavoud returned to court three months later with a letter from a therapist, indicating he had been undergoing treatment. This time, a different psychiatrist examined him but wrote at the end of his report, "Inconclusive: I have no opinion." The psychiatrist suggested that the case be referred back to the initial doctor so she could interview Mr. Poordavoud's therapist and obtain the full file from his hospitalization.

The judge, however, granted Mr. Poordavoud's restoration request that same day in a pro forma hearing.

In late 2004, Mr. Poordavoud drove up to a house in Chatsworth, Calif., in the middle of the night and began banging on the windows and the doors, shouting for an acquaintance to come out, according to court testimony.

When a man opened the door, Mr. Poordavoud sprayed him and two others with mace, according to court testimony. In the ensuing fight, Mr. Poordavoud slashed at one of them with a pair of brass knuckles fitted with blades.

Mr. Poordavoud retrieved a gun from his car and fired a single shot that missed. In an interview, he said he had only fired in the air in self-defense.

The police eventually charged Mr. Poordavoud with multiple felonies. He pleaded guilty to assault with a deadly weapon and using tear gas not in self-defense, and he was sentenced to about a year in county jail.

"I had an anger problem," said Mr. Poordavoud, who is no longer allowed to have guns because of his felony record. "I still have an anger problem."

Violence against others is not the only concern.

Ryan Anthony, the talented but troubled Disney artist who had a history of alcoholism, had talked about suicide for years with relatives. His father, Michael Anthony, said his son once threatened to jump off a highway overpass; another time, he vowed to hang himself from a chandelier in his home. A few months before he filed his petition to restore his firearms rights, he had attempted suicide by swallowing some pills, said his brother Loren.

But Mr. Anthony was able to hide his troubled past when a court-appointed psychiatrist examined him for the restoration hearing in April 2002. He told Dr. Rose Pitt, according to court records, that he had simply been going through a difficult period after he lost his job and split up with his wife. He was normally not a drinker, he said, but began drinking heavily. Since his involuntary hospitalization in mid-2001, he had been sober and attending Alcoholics Anonymous meetings, Dr. Pitt wrote in her report.

"Does not own guns but wants to skeet shoot, and so wants to purchase guns," Dr. Pitt wrote. "There does not appear to be any contraindication to his being able to get guns."

His relatives were incredulous. Had they been called, they said, they would have told officials to deny his request.

"I would have said, 'No, that doesn't sound right,' " Loren Anthony said. "He didn't like guns."

Mr. Anthony had been staying with Steven and Sofia Shafit, family friends. They said he had been doing better but was still hurting.

About two weeks after he got his firearms rights restored, he borrowed $300 from Ms. Shafit, saying he wanted to take a girl on a date. Instead, he went out and bought a shotgun — investigators found the receipt by his body — and checked into a room at a Holiday Inn.

On the desk, he left a three-page suicide note, according to a report from the Los Angeles County coroner's office. At some point, he lay down on the bed, placed the barrel of the shotgun in his mouth and pulled the trigger.

TOBY LYLES, **LISA SCHWARTZ** and **JACK STYCZYNSKI** contributed research.

Felons Finding It Easy to Regain Gun Rights

BY MICHAEL LUO | NOV. 13, 2011

IN FEBRUARY 2005, Erik Zettergren came home from a party after midnight with his girlfriend and another couple. They had all been drinking heavily, and soon the other man and Mr. Zettergren's girlfriend passed out on his bed. When Mr. Zettergren went to check on them later, he found his girlfriend naked from the waist down and the other man, Jason Robinson, with his pants around his ankles.

Enraged, Mr. Zettergren ordered Mr. Robinson to leave. After a brief confrontation, Mr. Zettergren shot him in the temple at point-blank range with a Glock-17 semiautomatic handgun. He then forced Mr. Robinson's hysterical fiancée, at gunpoint, to help him dispose of the body in a nearby river.

It was the first homicide in more than 30 years in the small town of Endicott, in eastern Washington. But for a judge's ruling two months before, it would probably never have happened.

For years, Mr. Zettergren had been barred from possessing firearms because of two felony convictions. He had a history of mental health problems and friends said he was dangerous. Yet Mr. Zettergren's gun rights were restored without even a hearing, under a state law that gave the judge no leeway to deny the application as long as certain basic requirements had been met. Mr. Zettergren, then 36, wasted no time retrieving several guns he had given to a friend for safekeeping.

"If he hadn't had his rights restored, in this particular instance, it probably would have saved the life of the other person," said Denis Tracy, the prosecutor in Whitman County, who handled the murder case.

Under federal law, people with felony convictions forfeit their right to bear arms. Yet every year, thousands of felons across the country have those rights reinstated, often with little or no review. In several states, they include people convicted of violent crimes, including first-degree murder and manslaughter, an examination by The New York Times has found.

While previously a small number of felons were able to reclaim their gun rights, the process became commonplace in many states in the late 1980s, after Congress started allowing state laws to dictate these reinstatements — part of an overhaul of federal gun laws orchestrated by the National Rifle Association. The restoration movement has gathered force in recent years, as gun rights advocates have sought to capitalize on the 2008 Supreme Court ruling that the Second Amendment protects an individual's right to bear arms.

This gradual pulling back of what many Americans have unquestioningly assumed was a blanket prohibition has drawn relatively little public notice. Indeed, state law enforcement agencies have scant information, if any, on which felons are getting their gun rights back, let alone how many have gone on to commit new crimes.

While many states continue to make it very difficult for felons to get their gun rights back — and federal felons are out of luck without a presidential pardon — many other jurisdictions are far more lenient, The Times found. In some, restoration is automatic for nonviolent felons as soon as they complete their sentences. In others, the decision is left up to judges, but the standards are generally vague, the process often perfunctory. In some states, even violent felons face a relatively low bar, with no waiting period before they can apply.

The Times examined hundreds of restoration cases in several states, among them Minnesota, where William James Holisky II, who had a history of stalking and terrorizing women, got his gun rights back last year, just six months after completing a three-year prison sentence for firing a shotgun into the house of a woman who had broken up with him after a handful of dates. She and her son were inside at the time of the shooting.

"My whole family's convinced that at some point he'll blow a gasket and that he'll come and shoot someone," said Vicky Holisky-Crets, Mr. Holisky's sister.

Also last year, a judge in Cleveland restored gun rights to Charles C. Hairston, who had been convicted of first-degree murder in North Carolina in 1971 for shooting a grocery store owner in the head with a shotgun. He also had another felony conviction, in 1995, for corruption of a minor.

Margaret C. Love, a pardon lawyer based in Washington, D.C., who has researched gun rights restoration laws, estimated that, depending on the type of crime, in more than half the states felons have a reasonable chance of getting back their gun rights.

That universe could well expand, as pro-gun groups shed a historical reluctance to advocate publicly for gun rights for felons. Lawyers litigating Second Amendment issues are also starting to challenge the more restrictive restoration laws. Pro-gun groups have pressed the issue in the last few years in states as diverse as Alaska, Ohio, Oregon and Tennessee.

Ohio's Legislature confronted the matter when it passed a law this year fixing a technicality that threatened to invalidate the state's restorations.

Ken Hanson, legislative chairman of the Buckeye Firearms Coalition, argued that felons should be able to reclaim their gun rights just as they can other civil rights.

"If it's a constitutional right, you treat it with equal dignity with other rights," he said.

But Toby Hoover, executive director of the Ohio Coalition Against Gun Violence, contended that the public was safer without guns in the hands of people who have committed serious crimes.

"It seems that Ohio legislators have plenty of problems to solve that should be a much higher priority than making sure criminals have guns," Ms. Hoover said in written testimony.

That question — whether the restorations pose a risk to public safety — has received little study, in part because data can be hard to come by.

The Times analyzed data from Washington State, where Mr. Zettergren had his gun rights restored. The most serious felons are barred, but otherwise judges have no discretion to reject the petitions, as long as the applicant fulfills certain criteria. (In 2003, a state appeals court panel stated that a petitioner "had no burden to show that he is safe to own or possess guns.")

Since 1995, more than 3,300 felons and people convicted of domestic violence misdemeanors have regained their gun rights in the state — 430 in 2010 alone — according to the analysis of data provided by the state police and the court system. Of that number, more than 400 — about 13 percent — have subsequently committed new crimes, the analysis found. More than 200 committed felonies, including murder, assault in the first and second degree, child rape and drive-by shooting.

Even some felons who have regained their firearms rights say the process needs to be more rigorous.

"It's kind of spooky, isn't it?" said Beau Krueger, who has two assaults on his record and got his gun rights back last year in Minnesota after only a brief hearing, in which local prosecutors did not even participate. "We could have all kinds of crazy hoodlums out here with guns that shouldn't have guns."

POWERFUL LOBBY PREVAILS

The federal firearms prohibition for felons dates to the late 1960s, when the assassinations of the Rev. Dr. Martin Luther King Jr. and Senator Robert F. Kennedy, along with rioting across the country, set off a clamor for stricter gun control laws. Congress enacted sweeping legislation that included a provision extending the firearms ban for convicted criminals beyond those who had committed "crimes of violence," a standard adopted in the 1930s.

"All of our people who are deeply concerned about law and order should hail this day," President Lyndon B. Johnson said upon signing the Gun Control Act in October 1968.

Even the N.R.A. backed the bill. But by the late 1970s, a more hard-line faction, committed to an expansive view of the Second Amendment, had taken control of the group. A crowning achievement was the Firearm Owners Protection Act of 1986, which significantly loosened federal gun laws.

When it came to felons' gun rights, the legislation essentially left the matter up to states. The federal gun restrictions would no longer apply if a state had restored a felon's civil rights — to vote, sit on a jury and hold public office — and the individual faced no other firearms prohibitions.

The restoration issue drew relatively little notice in the Congressional battle over the bill. But officials of the federal Bureau of Alcohol, Tobacco and Firearms identified the provision in an internal memo as among their serious concerns. Some state law enforcement officials also sounded the alarm.

When Senator David F. Durenberger, a Minnesota Republican, realized after the law passed that thousands of felons, including those convicted of violent crimes, in his state would suddenly be getting their gun rights back, he sought the N.R.A.'s help in rolling back the provision. Doug Kelley, his chief of staff at the time, thought the group would "surely want to close this loophole."

But the senator, Mr. Kelley recalled, "ran into a stone wall," as the N.R.A. threatened to pull its support for him if he did not drop the matter, which he eventually did.

"The N.R.A. slammed the door on us," Mr. Kelley said. "That absolutely baffled me."

Until then, the avenues for restoration had been narrow and few: a direct appeal to the federal firearms agency, which conducted detailed background investigations; a state pardon expressly authorizing gun possession, or a presidential pardon. Felons convicted of crimes involving guns or other weapons, as well as those convicted of violating federal gun laws, were expressly barred from applying to the federal firearms agency.

By contrast, the restoration of civil rights, which is now central to regaining gun rights, is relatively routine, automatic in many states upon completion of a sentence. In some states, felons must also petition for a judicial order specifically restoring firearms rights. Other potential paths include a pardon from the governor or state clemency board or a "set aside" — essentially, an annulment — of the conviction.

Today, in at least 11 states, including Kansas, Ohio, Minnesota and Rhode Island, restoration of firearms rights is automatic, without any review at all, for many nonviolent felons, usually once they finish their sentences, or after a certain amount of time crime-free. Even violent felons may petition to have their firearms rights restored in states like Ohio, Minnesota and Virginia. Some states, including Georgia and Nebraska, award scores of pardons every year that specifically confer gun privileges.

Felons face steep odds, though, in states like California, where the governor's office gives out only a handful of pardons every year, if that.

"It's a long, drawn-out process," said Steve Lindley, chief of the State Department of Justice's firearms bureau. "They were convicted of a felony crime. There are penalties for that."

Studies on the impact of gun restrictions largely support barring felons from possessing firearms.

One study, published in the American Journal of Public Health in 1999, found that denying handgun purchases to felons cut their risk of committing new gun or violent crimes by 20 to 30 percent. A year earlier, a study in the Journal of the American Medical Association found that handgun purchasers with at least one prior misdemeanor — not even a felony — were more than seven times as likely as those with no criminal history to be charged with new offenses over a 15-year period.

Criminologists studying recidivism have found that felons usually have to stay out of trouble for about a decade before their risk of committing a crime equals that of people with no records. According to Alfred Blumstein, a professor at Carnegie Mellon University, for violent offenders, that period is 11 to 15 years; for drug offenders, 10 to 14 years; and for those who have committed property crimes, 8 to 11 years. An important caveat: Professor Blumstein did not look at what happens when felons are given guns.

The history of the federal firearms agency's own restoration program, though, offers reason for caution. The program came under attack in the early 1990s, when the Violence Policy Center, a gun control group, discovered that dozens of felons granted restorations over a five-year period had been arrested again, including some on charges of attempted murder and sexual assault. (The center also found that many of those granted gun rights were felons convicted of violent or drug-related crimes.) In the resulting uproar and over the objections of the N.R.A., Congress killed the program.

A SUPERFICIAL PROCESS

In 2001, three police officers in the Columbia Heights suburb of Minneapolis were shot and wounded by a convicted murderer whose firearms rights had been restored automatically in 1987, 10 years after he completed a six-and-a-half year prison sentence and then probation for killing his estranged wife and a family friend with a shotgun. (The State Legislature had imposed the 10-year waiting period for violent felons after it discovered what Senator Durenberger had feared: that felons' gun rights would be restored immediately under the Firearm Owners Protection Act.)

What happened in the wake of the shooting is emblematic of how the issue has played out in many states, particularly where the gun lobby is powerful.

Two Democratic legislators sought to impose a lifetime firearms ban on violent felons, although they concluded that for their bills to have any chance of passing, they would also have to set up a process that held out a hope of eventual restoration. They were unable, however, to get their bills through the Legislature.

The issue was taken up the following year by Republican lawmakers, but it became wrapped up in legislation to relax concealed-weapons laws. Initially, a moderate Republican introduced a bill with a 5- to 10-year waiting period for regaining gun rights, but the waiting period was scrapped entirely in the law, written by gun-rights advocates, that was finally enacted in 2003. That law, which does not even mandate that prosecutors be notified of the hearings, requires judges to grant the requests merely if the petitioners show "good cause."

"The decision was, we have good judges and we trust them," said Joseph Olson, who helped write the statute as president of the advocacy group Concealed Carry Reform Now.

One man who has benefited from a Minnesota judge's gun rights ruling is William Holisky.

Mr. Holisky, an accountant who has struggled with bipolar disorder and alcoholism, had gone out only a few times with Karen Roman, a nurse he had met online, before she broke up with him.

In August 2006, Ms. Roman was getting ready to work a night shift, putting on makeup in the bathroom of her home in Duluth, when she heard a truck pulling up and a loud boom. Moments later, she heard another boom and glass breaking. She hit the floor, calling out to her teenage son in the other room to do the same as she crawled to the phone to dial 911.

The police arrested Mr. Holisky later that night for drunken driving. Several months later, they charged him in the shooting as well. He pleaded guilty to second-degree assault with a dangerous weapon.

Around the same time, he also pleaded guilty to a felony charge of making terroristic threats against an elderly neighbor. The woman had reported to the police that someone — she suspected Mr. Holisky — had left her a threatening and obscene note. She had also reported a series of escalating incidents that included harassing telephone calls, his entering her apartment and someone's smashing her bedroom window. Mr. Holisky also had a misdemeanor burglary conviction from 2003, for breaking into an ex-girlfriend's house, as well as another misdemeanor conviction for violating an order of protection.

In Mr. Holisky's gun rights hearing in October 2010 in Two Harbors, a small town on the north shore of Lake Superior, Russell Conrow, the prosecutor in Lake County, argued that Mr. Holisky had not yet proved that he could stay clean, given that he had just gotten out of prison. Mr. Conrow also pointed out that there were two active orders of protection against Mr. Holisky.

"There were people still scared of him," Mr. Conrow said recently.

For his part, Mr. Holisky took documents from the plea agreement in his assault case, in which the prosecutor in neighboring St. Louis County agreed not to oppose the restoration of his firearms rights.

Mr. Holisky, who is 59, did not specify in his often-rambling petition exactly why he wanted a gun. He described his behavior in 2006 as an "aberration."

The county judge, Kenneth Sandvik, was set to retire in a few months. He knew Mr. Holisky's family from growing up in the community. Several weeks later, he ruled that Mr. Holisky had met the basic requirements of the law.

In an interview, Judge Sandvik said he had given considerable weight to the St. Louis County prosecutor's agreement not to oppose the restoration of gun rights for Mr. Holisky. But Gary Bjorklund, an assistant St. Louis County attorney, said in an interview that he had been focused on extracting a guilty plea that would send Mr. Holisky to prison and had thought no judge would take a firearms request from Mr. Holisky seriously.

Judge Sandvik acknowledged that he had not looked into the details of Mr. Holisky's assault case, arguing that his job had been only to review what the prosecutor had presented to him.

"We're not investigators," he said.

The ease with which Mr. Holisky regained his gun rights does not appear to be an anomaly. Using partial data from Minnesota's Judicial Branch, The Times identified more than 70 cases since 2004 of people convicted of "crimes of violence" who have gotten their gun rights back. A closer look at a number of them found a superficial process. The cases included those of Mr. Krueger, who criticized the system as insufficiently rigorous after winning back his gun rights in a perfunctory hearing, and of another man whose petition was approved without even a hearing, even though his felony involved pulling a gun on a man.

The ruling in Mr. Holisky's case prompted members of his family to write a series of frantic e-mails to Judge Sandvik and Mr. Conrow, warning of dire consequences.

It is not entirely clear whether Mr. Holisky, who did not respond to several requests for comment, is legally able to buy a gun at this point, because at least one of the outstanding orders of protection, which expires next year, appears to trip another federal prohibition. But Mr. Holisky has been writing letters to relatives in Texas, threatening legal action if they do not turn over his gun collection.

So far, they have refused.

A KILLER'S SUCCESSFUL PETITION

Just as in Minnesota, violent felons in Ohio are allowed to apply for restoration of firearms rights after completing their sentences. The statute is similarly vague, requiring only that a judge find that the petitioner has "led a law-abiding life since discharge or release, and appears likely to do so."

Only a handful of county clerks in Ohio said they could track these cases, producing records on several dozen restorations. They included people who had been convicted of first-degree murder, voluntary manslaughter, felonious assault and sexual battery.

The case of Charles Hairston in Cuyahoga County stands out.

Mr. Hairston was 17 in January 1971, when he shot a man to death in Winston-Salem, N.C. Mr. Hairston and a group of neighborhood toughs had been preparing to rob a local grocery store when the owner, Charles Minor, 55, closed up and headed for his car.

"I am fixing to get him," Mr. Hairston told one of his friends, according to witness statements to the police, before he pulled the trigger on a 20-gauge shotgun.

Mr. Hairston spent 18 years in prison before being released on parole in 1989. He moved to Cleveland and started working in heating and cooling, a trade he had learned behind bars.

In 1995, he pleaded no contest to a misdemeanor charge for allegedly grabbing and pushing his wife.

More seriously, later that year he was indicted on 60 counts of rape, felonious sexual penetration and gross sexual imposition; prosecutors charged that he had forced sex upon his stepdaughter, starting when she was 12. He was acquitted of the most serious charges and convicted only of corruption of a minor for one encounter at a motel for which prosecutors were able to provide corroborating evidence beyond the girl's detailed testimony.

Mr. Hairston, who denies the charges and is still fighting the conviction, filed his first gun rights restoration application in 2006 in Cuyahoga County but was summarily denied.

When he filed a new petition two years later, a judge thought he was ineligible and denied him again, though she wrote in her decision that she did not believe Mr. Hairston was likely to break the law again. But an appeals court ruled that the judge had misread the statute, and sent the case back for another hearing late last year.

The county prosecutor's office had vigorously opposed the restoration from the beginning. But Mr. Hairston, who took in several friends as character witnesses, told the judge he had grown up in prison.

"Nearly 40 years ago, you know, I was a dumb kid," Mr. Hairston said at his first hearing. He added, "I am in a situation now where if, God forbid, if someone was to come into my home and attack me, my wife, there isn't a lot I could say about it, there isn't a lot I could do."

In the end, the judge, Hollie L. Gallagher, granted his petition without comment.

Soon after the judge's ruling, Mr. Hairston obtained a concealed weapons permit from a neighboring county and bought a 9-millimeter semiautomatic handgun.

RETURNING TO CRIME

Erik Zettergren originally lost his gun rights in 1987 because of a felony conviction for dealing marijuana. A decade later, the police went to his house after being called by his ex-wife and discovered a cache of guns. He was convicted of another felony, unlawful possession of a firearm.

He relinquished his weapons to friends but eventually got them back, sometimes hiding them in an old car in his backyard, according to friends. Sometime after that, though, he became worried that the police might come after him again and turned over the guns — two long guns and a Glock pistol — to a friend, Tom Williams.

"I kept them under my bed," Mr. Williams said.

In December 2004, Mr. Zettergren successfully petitioned in Kittitas County — a three-hour drive from his home — to have his gun rights restored. (Like Minnesota's, Washington's law allows petitioners to apply anywhere.) Court records show he did not even have a hearing. Instead, his lawyer, Paul T. Ferris, who specializes in these cases, took care of the matter.

Right away, Mr. Zettergren retrieved his guns from Mr. Williams and soon obtained a concealed pistol license. He made something of a sport of showing off his Glock to friends. "He was so proud of that thing," said Larry Persons, a friend. "He was flashing it in front of everybody."

Not long after, he would use it in the killing.

Washington's gun rights restoration statute dates to a 1995 statewide initiative, the Hard Times for Armed Crimes Act, that toughened penalties for crimes involving firearms. The initiative was spearheaded, in part, by pro-gun activists, including leaders of the Second Amendment Foundation, an advocacy group, and the N.R.A.

Although it drew little notice at the time, the legislation also included an expansion of what had been very limited eligibility for restoration of firearms rights.

"There were a lot of people who we felt should be able to get their gun rights restored who could not," said Alan M. Gottlieb, founder of the Second Amendment Foundation, who was active in the effort.

Under the legislation, "Class A" felons — who have committed the most serious crimes, like murder and manslaughter — are ineligible, as are sex offenders. Otherwise, judges are required to grant the petitions as long as, essentially, felons have not been convicted of any new crimes in the five years after completing their sentences. Judges have no discretion to deny the requests based upon character, mental health or any other factors. Mr. Gottlieb said they explicitly wrote the statute this way.

"We were having problems with judges that weren't going to restore rights no matter what," he said.

The statute's mix of strictness and leniency makes Washington a useful testing ground.

The Times's analysis found that among the more than 400 people who committed crimes after winning back their gun rights under the new law, more than 70 committed Class A or B felonies. Over all, more than 80 were convicted of some sort of assault and more than 100 of drug offenses.

There were cases like that of Mitchell W. Reed, disqualified from possessing firearms after a 1984 felony cocaine conviction. He also has seven misdemeanor convictions on his record from the 1980s, including for assault. In 2003, he successfully petitioned for his gun rights in Snohomish County Superior Court.

His wife, Debi Reed, went with him to the hearing and said in an interview that she had been shocked at how easily his rights were restored. He immediately bought a 9-millimeter semiautomatic handgun.

The following year, she said, he beat her up for the first time. In 2008 he became more angry and violent, she said, in one instance putting a gun in her hand during an argument, pointing it at his head and saying he was going to frame her for murder. During another fight that year, he struck her with a gun, giving her a black eye, and held a loaded gun to her head.

Mr. Reed was ultimately arrested in 2009 and charged with harassing and threatening to kill his wife's ex-husband. While those charges were pending, he was arrested on second-degree assault charges after he beat up and tried to strangle his wife. The charging documents also mentioned the 2008 gun episode. He eventually pleaded guilty to third-degree assault and intimidating a witness, as well as fourth-degree assault and harassment.

Jason C. Keller, disqualified because of a 1997 burglary conviction, had his rights restored after a brief hearing in 2006. He waited a few years before buying a Hi-Point .40-caliber semiautomatic pistol, according to his girlfriend at the time, Shawna Braylock. But she did not trust him with the gun because of his temper, making him keep it at his parents' house.

In 2010, Mr. Keller left a Fourth of July party in the late evening, picked up his gun and drove to the house of a woman he knew. He fired several shots as she stood out front with her 9-year-old son; her 6-year-old daughter was sleeping inside. Mr. Keller pleaded guilty to drive-by shooting, a felony.

In Mr. Zettergren's case, his friends said they were shocked that a judge had restored his gun rights, because they knew he was receiving disability payments, in part because of mental health problems.

"Most of the people around here that knew him, knew that he could be dangerous," said Darrell Reinhardt, one of Mr. Zettergren's friends.

Mr. Zettergren's mental health issues, in fact, have been at the heart of his efforts to appeal his convictions for second-degree murder, second-degree assault and unlawful imprisonment. He had been in counseling since 2000, and several mental health experts had found he had post-traumatic stress disorder and major depression, saying he had a "very high degree of psychological disturbance" and suffered frequent "flashbacks and disturbing images," according to a declaration from a forensic psychologist in one of Mr. Zettergren's appeal briefs. The post-traumatic stress, according to the psychologist, resulted from scenes he had witnessed years before, including his mother's death by electrocution and the shooting death of a friend.

None of this was reviewed by the judge who heard Mr. Zettergren's gun rights petition.

Donna Bly, the mother of Jason Robinson, Mr. Zettergren's shooting victim, considered suing the county for negligence over the decision but could not find a lawyer to take the case. She also tried bringing the issue up with a state legislator but got nowhere.

"This man did not deserve to have his gun rights back," she said.

TOBY LYLES and **LISA SCHWARTZ** contributed research. **TOM TOROK** contributed reporting.

Answers on Felons and Gun Rights

BY MICHAEL LUO | NOV. 15, 2011

On Tuesday, the reporter Michael Luo of The Times is answering reader questions prompted by his recent article on how easy it is in many states for people with felony convictions to get their gun rights reinstated.

Q: *Which are the five states where it is easiest to get gun rights restored? And which are the five where it is most difficult? — CJGC, Cambridge, Mass.*

A: A lot of people have asked questions about specific states. It is hard to provide a complete 50-state rundown because all of these laws are complicated and often obscure. But let me try to take at least a partial stab at answering your question. In terms of the states where it is easiest for felons to get their gun rights back, you would have to start with the cluster of states that restore at least some felons' firearms rights automatically upon completion of their sentences.

In Minnesota, for instance, non-violent felons regain their firearms rights when they complete their sentences. People who have committed a "crime of violence" must petition in court to have their rights restored. The law, however, does not require that prosecutors be notified; petitioners can apply anywhere, so they can, theoretically, shop around for friendly judges; and there is no waiting period. Applicants are merely required to show "good cause." Besides the cases I mentioned in the article from Minnesota, I came across another in which someone who had been convicted of second degree assault for pulling a gun on another man got his firearms rights back without even having to show up in court.

I also cited cases out of Ohio for the article, including that of a first degree murderer who had his gun rights restored. Ohio is another state where non-violent felons can possess firearms upon completion of their sentences. Violent felons are barred but can petition in court. The state's statute requires that a judge find that the petitioner has "led a law-abiding life since discharge or release, and appears likely to do so." I reviewed several dozen restorations of gun rights in Ohio, including cases in which people had been convicted of voluntary manslaughter, sexual battery and felonious assault.

In Montana, the only felons who are not allowed to have firearms when they complete their sentences are those who used a dangerous weapon in their crime. Even these people, however, can petition in court to have their firearms rights restored. In North Dakota, even felons whose offense involved "violence or intimidation" automatically regain their firearms rights 10 years after completion of their sentences.

I did less research on states where it is hardest to get gun rights reinstated. These would have to be states where a pardon is the only route, and they are generally difficult to get. California is one state I mentioned in the article. The governor's office granted only nine pardons last year; in 2009, it granted only two.

Falling somewhere in between are states like Georgia and Nebraska, in which pardons are the only route to restoring firearms rights for felons, but they are also fairly readily available. Georgia's State Board of Pardons and Paroles, for instance, granted nearly 200 pardons explicitly restoring the right to bear arms in 2010, including for people convicted of voluntary manslaughter, homicide by vehicle, aggravated child molestation and armed robbery, according to records I obtained through a public records request. Last fiscal year, the Nebraska Board of Pardons granted 100 pardons that specifically restored firearms rights, according to data provided by the board.

Washington State, which was featured prominently in the article, is another state that might fall somewhere in the middle on the scale of strictness. It bars the most serious felons, those convicted of Class A felonies, but judges essentially are required to restore gun rights to anyone who applies after going five years without another conviction.

There is no room for discretion to deny petitions based upon character, or mental health, or any other factors.

Q: *I'm decidedly pro-firearms, and also pro-sane and reasonable regulation. Now let's look at this article: "That question — whether the restorations pose a risk to public safety — has received little study, in part because data can be hard to come by." But not anecdotal tales of terror and mayhem. These are in ample supply, apparently, and are strategically placed throughout this story. Then, in the very next paragraphs, you cite various analyses of tons of data, which you just said could be hard to come by. Which is it? — Eric R., Tucson, Ariz.*

A: Data on who gets firearms rights restored are, indeed, hard to come by. Law enforcement agencies generally do not systematically track these restorations. In Ohio, for example, I checked with various state agencies and came up empty. Instead, I had to e-mail the county clerks in all 88 counties in the state to ask if they had ability to track these court restorations. Most said they could not, but a few could and were able to produce records for several dozen restorations.

You mentioned data I cited out of Washington State. I assume you are referring to this passage: "Since 1995, more than 3,300 felons and people convicted of domestic violence misdemeanors have regained their gun rights in the state — 430 in 2010 alone — according to the analysis of data provided by the state police and the court system. Of that number, more than 400 — about 13 percent — have subsequently committed new crimes, the analysis found. More than 200 committed felonies, including murder, assault in the first and second degree, child rape and drive-by shooting."

This data actually took months of effort to obtain. Initially, I got a list of restorations dating to the 1990s from programmers at the state Administrative Office of the Courts. But this turned out to be only a partial list. The Washington State Patrol records these restorations in its criminal history database, but officials there refused to turn over their database to me. In the end, I negotiated with the state police officials, and they agreed to provide me with data with no names attached. I had asked them if they could calculate a recidivism rate for me, but they were unable to do so because of the way the dates of the restorations were listed in their database. But I was able to work with one of our computer assisted reporting gurus, Tom Torok, to extract those dates. After that, I ran a query against conviction data I got from the police and the courts to see how many had committed crimes after they got their firearms rights restored.

Q: *I was wondering if you were aware of the unreliability of certain kinds of recidivism data. The data becomes increasingly unreliable the more minor the crime. There is an almost machine like automation by which persons charged with infractions and misdemeanors are arrested again. The statistic from the A.M.A. that you quoted is the re-arrest rate for the innocent as well as criminal, regardless of conviction. — NYC*

A: I e-mailed Dr. Garen J. Wintemute, director of the Violence Prevention Research Program at the University of California, Davis, and the lead author of that study you cited, to respond to your question. The study, which was published in The Journal of the American Medical Association, found that handgun buyers with at least one misdemeanor were more than seven times as likely as those with no criminal history to be charged with new offenses over a 15-year period. The risk for those with multiple such convictions was 10 times greater.

Dr. Wintemute acknowledged that the re-arrest rate as measurement of new criminal activity "is not a perfect measure." The alternative is to use only conviction data. But Dr. Wintemute said the risk of a "false positive" by declaring that new criminal activity had occurred, based on a new arrest, without reference to the disposition of the case, is lower than the risk of a "false negative" by declaring that no new criminal activity had occurred based solely on conviction data. He added, this is particularly true when the period of follow-up is short, as dispositions for new offenses may not be available by the time follow-up ends.

I should point out that in my own crunching of data on restorations of firearms rights in Washington State, I used conviction data to come up with the figure that roughly 13 percent of people who had gotten their gun rights restored re-offended.

Q: *Did any of the court cases you researched specifically rule that the right to bear arms was also a right of a felon? — Sarah H., NYC*

A: You are actually raising an issue that lawyers told me is an emerging area of Second Amendment litigation. The Supreme Court ruled in 2008 in District of Columbia v. Heller that the Second Amendment protected the individual's right to bear arms. Justice Antonin Scalia wrote, however, that the court's opinion "should not be taken to cast doubt on longstanding prohibitions on the possession of firearms by felons" and others. Nevertheless, lawyers have begun to try to chip away at this prohibition in individual cases, particularly when it comes to people convicted of non-violent felonies, arguing that the federal ban on all felons, as opposed to only violent ones, from possessing firearms dates back only a few decades. They have also argued that the Supreme Court ruled the right to bear arms is closely tied to the right to self-defense. It is a legal area worth watching in the next few years.

Q: *Is this the law in New York? — Alice Printz, New York*

A: There is a complicated answer for New York, which is partly why my editors and I decided not to include it in the story. While reporting the story, I repeatedly turned to Margaret Love, a pardon lawyer based in Washington, D.C., who is the authority on various state laws and how they interact with the federal law.

According to information provided by her, as well as officials from the New York State Department of Corrections and Supervision, in New York, felons who want to possess firearms must obtain a Certificate of Good Conduct that expressly restores their firearms rights either from the Board of Parole or their sentencing court. Anyone who has been convicted of a violent felony or a Class A1 felony is barred. I obtained through a Freedom of Information Law request records on certificates issued by the Board of Parole. There were 17 issued in 2010 and 36 in 2009. I did not find out how many are issued by the courts.

Here is the problem: The Board of Parole issues many certificates that specifically identify what type of firearms the convicted felon is allowed to possess — long guns only, for instance, or handguns only. The federal law basically says that if a felon's civil rights have been restored — meaning the right to vote, sit on a jury and hold public office — and there are no other restrictions on the person having a firearm, then they are no longer disqualified federally from possessing guns. The right to vote is restored in New York automatically upon expiration of sentence or discharge from parole; the Certificate of Good Conduct restores the other civil rights. But courts have ruled that if a state bars someone from having any type of firearm — say a person is only allowed to have long guns-then they are barred federally from having any firearms at all. In other words, these people may actually be allowed to have guns under New York State law, but they may, technically, be in violation of the federal law still.

Yes, very confusing.

Q: *It's possible for a convicted criminal to own a firearm but this same person doesn't have the right to vote? — Mark F., Glen Oaks, N.Y.*

A: Let me clear this up, because it is a detail that many seem to have missed. Under federal law, in a word, the answer is, "No." The federal law that governs whether felons can possess firearms says that they are barred, unless their civil rights have been restored by their state, and there are no other prohibitions against them having firearms. Courts have held that the civil rights that must be restored are the right to vote, sit on a jury and hold public office. In other words, if they can have a firearm under federal law, they, by definition, have had their right to vote restored.

There is a bit of confusion, however, when it comes to state law. Some states, for example, restore firearms privileges, without some of these rights having been restored. These people, then, may be allowed to have a gun under state law, but federal law actually holds sway, and they could then be arrested and charged as a felon in possession by federal authorities.

The Gun Rights Tilt

OPINION | BY ROSS DOUTHAT | JULY 24, 2012

PRESIDENT OBAMA HAS staked out some surprisingly liberal positions during this campaign season. From gay marriage to illegal immigration, the White House has deliberately created stark contrasts with the Republican Party on ground where Democratic politicians have often been on defense.

But not on gun control. As with previous tragedies, last Friday's massacre in Aurora, Colo., inspired a groundswell of op-eds and blog posts making the case for stricter gun laws. But the president conspicuously failed to embrace this argument. The White House's official statement on the issue, offered by Jay Carney, Obama's press secretary, reaffirmed the president's support for the "Second Amendment rights of the American people" while urging more effective enforcement of gun laws as they exist today.

This caution is not surprising, given the public's distinctly anti-gun control tilt. The tilt itself, though, has not been adequately explained. The American love affair with guns and gun culture is deep and enduring, but 20 years ago it coexisted with broad support for more restrictions on how and when and whether weapons could be bought and sold.

In 1990, Gallup reported almost 80 percent support for the proposition that gun laws should become "more strict." By 2010, though, just 44 percent of Americans wanted stricter gun laws, compared to 54 percent who opposed them. That's a striking swing for such a short time period.

Some writers have pinned this shift on the timorousness of Democratic politicians, who were spooked by the N.R.A.'s ability to mobilize gun owners behind Republicans in the 1994 election and have simply given up the fight. In this account, there's still a potentially pro-gun-control majority, visible in polls that ask questions about specific kinds of gun restrictions. It's just waiting to be mobilized by a more courageous generation of liberal politicians than the ones we have today.

Another possibility, raised at CNN.com by the conservative columnist David Frum, is that notwithstanding years of falling crime rates, the "if it bleeds it leads" approach taken by television news has persuaded Americans that their country is actually getting much more dangerous, and that they need guns to protect themselves from a (mythical) crime wave washing through the streets.

These arguments have some merit, but the first one probably gives too little credit to the political instincts of Democratic lawmakers, and the second one probably credits the 11 o'clock news with more influence than it actually exerts. If local news really misled Americans so completely, one would expect crime to be a much higher-salience issue in our politics than it's been these last two decades.

Let me suggest two other factors that may play a role in gun control's collapsing support. The first is the actual collapse in crime rates since 1990. As Frum suggests, for some Americans the fear of crime drives support for gun ownership. But for others, it presumably drives support for gun restrictions: In a time when public order seems precarious, they're a "tough on crime" measure that even liberals can love.

In this reading of history, it isn't surprising that the Democratic Party's support for gun control peaked when the crime rate was peaking. Recall that the assault weapons ban was part of Bill Clinton's 1994 sweeping crime bill, which was supposed to inoculate his party against Republican law-and-order attacks. Nor is it surprising that the appeal of gun restrictions ebbed as other methods of crime fighting — more police, better policing, mass incarceration — produced a substantial drop in crime rates.

It is also not surprising that shocking episodes like the Aurora shooting (or Virginia Tech, or Columbine) haven't reversed this trend. Whatever their views on gun rights, most Americans are sensible enough to realize that if gun restrictions reduce crime at all — and the evidence on this point is murky at best — they are probably least effective at deterring would-be mass murderers, who tend, like James

Holmes with his homemade bombs, to be highly adaptable in their choice of weaponry.

A second factor driving declining support for gun control, meanwhile, is a trend in our politics, inherent to American life but particularly potent since the social revolutions of the 1960s, for rights-based arguments to carry the day over more communitarian appeals.

This tendency cuts across the usual lines of left and right. We tend to associate gun control with social liberalism, but the same trends that have buoyed public support for gay marriage and marijuana legalization have also encouraged a more expansive reading of the Second Amendment.

The common thread is our increasing individualism, and the triumph of rights-talk over other forms of moral and political argument. The gun-rights movement talks about the rights of "law-abiding citizens" the way the gay rights movement talks about the freedoms of "consenting adults," and while the arguments play to different audiences they have a very American premise in common.

In this sense, the gun control debate offers liberals a chance to experience something that social conservatives often feel: The mix of confusion and alienation that comes with sensing that your country has somehow slipped away from you, and that your convictions don't have a place in the unfolding of the American idea.

ROSS DOUTHAT is an Op-Ed columnist for The New York Times.

In Gun Debate, a Misguided Focus on Mental Illness

COLUMN | BY RICHARD A. FRIEDMAN, M.D. | DEC. 17, 2012

IN THE WAKE of the terrible shooting at an elementary school in Newtown, Conn., national attention has turned again to the complex links between violence, mental illness and gun control.

The gunman, Adam Lanza, 20, has been described as a loner who was intelligent and socially awkward. And while no official diagnosis has been made public, armchair diagnosticians have been quick to assert that keeping guns from getting into the hands of people with mental illness would help solve the problem of gun homicides.

Arguing against stricter gun-control measures, Representative Mike Rogers, Republican of Michigan and a former F.B.I. agent, said, "What the more realistic discussion is, 'How do we target people with mental illness who use firearms?' "

Robert A. Levy, chairman of the Cato Institute, told The New York Times: "To reduce the risk of multivictim violence, we would be better advised to focus on early detection and treatment of mental illness."

But there is overwhelming epidemiological evidence that the vast majority of people with psychiatric disorders do not commit violent acts. Only about 4 percent of violence in the United States can be attributed to people with mental illness.

This does not mean that mental illness is not a risk factor for violence. It is, but the risk is actually small. Only certain serious psychiatric illnesses are linked to an increased risk of violence.

One of the largest studies, the National Institute of Mental Health's Epidemiologic Catchment Area study, which followed nearly 18,000 subjects, found that the lifetime prevalence of violence among people with serious mental illness — like schizophrenia and bipolar disorder — was 16 percent, compared with 7 percent among people without any mental disorder. Anxiety disorders, in contrast, do not seem to increase the risk at all.

Alcohol and drug abuse are far more likely to result in violent behavior than mental illness by itself. In the National Institute of Mental Health's E.C.A. study, for example, people with no mental disorder who abused alcohol or drugs were nearly seven times as likely as those without substance abuse to commit violent acts.

It's possible that preventing people with schizophrenia, bipolar disorder and other serious mental illnesses from getting guns might decrease the risk of mass killings. Even the Supreme Court, which in 2008 strongly affirmed a broad right to bear arms, at the same time endorsed prohibitions on gun ownership "by felons and the mentally ill."

But mass killings are very rare events, and because people with mental illness contribute so little to overall violence, these measures would have little impact on everyday firearm-related killings. Consider that between 2001 and 2010, there were nearly 120,000 gun-related homicides, according to the National Center for Health Statistics. Few were perpetrated by people with mental illness.

Perhaps more significant, we are not very good at predicting who is likely to be dangerous in the future. According to Dr. Michael Stone, professor of clinical psychiatry at Columbia and an expert on mass murderers, "Most of these killers are young men who are not floridly psychotic. They tend to be paranoid loners who hold a grudge and are full of rage."

Even though we know from large-scale epidemiologic studies like the E.C.A. study that a young psychotic male who is intoxicated with alcohol and has a history of involuntary commitment is at a high risk of violence, most individuals who fit this profile are harmless.

Jeffrey Swanson, a professor of psychiatry at Duke University and a leading expert in the epidemiology of violence, said in an e-mail, "Can we reliably predict violence? 'No' is the short answer. Psychiatrists, using clinical judgment, are not much better than chance at predicting which individual patients will do something violent and which will not."

It would be even harder to predict a mass shooting, Dr. Swanson said, "You can profile the perpetrators after the fact and you'll get a description of troubled young men, which also matches the description of thousands of other troubled young men who would never do something like this."

Even if clinicians could predict violence perfectly, keeping guns from people with mental illness is easier said than done. Nearly five years after Congress enacted the National Instant Criminal Background Check System, only about half of the states have submitted more than a tiny proportion of their mental health records.

How effective are laws that prohibit people with mental illness from obtaining guns? According to Dr. Swanson's recent research, these measures may prevent some violent crime. But, he added, "there are a lot of people who are undeterred by these laws."

Adam Lanza was prohibited from purchasing a gun, because he was too young. Yet he managed to get his hands on guns — his mother's — anyway. If we really want to stop young men like him from becoming mass murderers, and prevent the small amount of violence attributable to mental illness, we should invest our resources in better screening for, and treatment of, psychiatric illness in young people.

All the focus on the small number of people with mental illness who are violent serves to make us feel safer by displacing and limiting the threat of violence to a small, well-defined group. But the sad and frightening truth is that the vast majority of homicides are carried out by outwardly normal people in the grip of all too ordinary human aggression to whom we provide nearly unfettered access to deadly force.

In the "Mind" column, **BENEDICT CAREY** and other contributors to Science Times take deeper looks at the latest news developments in psychiatry, psychology and neuroscience.

Don't Blame Mental Illness for Gun Violence

EDITORIAL | BY THE NEW YORK TIMES | DEC. 15, 2015

THOSE WHO OPPOSE expanded gun-control legislation frequently argue that instead of limiting access to guns, the country should focus on mental health problems.

"People with mental illness are getting guns and committing these mass shootings," said Paul Ryan, the speaker of the House, after the shooting in San Bernardino, Calif., early this month. And Republicans in the Senate backed mental-health legislation even as they rejected bills to require universal background checks and bar people on the terrorism watch list from buying guns.

But mass shootings represent a small percentage of all gun violence, and mental illness is not a factor in most violent acts. According to one epidemiological estimate, entirely eliminating the effects of mental illness would reduce all violence by only 4 percent. Over all, less than 5 percent of gun homicides between 2001 and 2010 were committed by people with diagnoses of mental illness, according to a public health study published this year.

Blaming mental health problems for gun violence in America gives the public the false impression that most people with mental illness are dangerous, when in fact a vast majority will never commit violence. Still, some legal changes should be made to reduce access to firearms among the small percentage of people with mental illness who are dangerous to themselves or others.

Estimates of the percentage of mass shooters who are mentally ill vary widely, as both "mass shooting" and "mental illness" can be difficult to define. One recent analysis of murderers who killed or intended to kill four or more people found that 22 percent of male killers exhibited evidence of mental illness (the share was higher among women, but the sample was much smaller). Another analysis, by the group

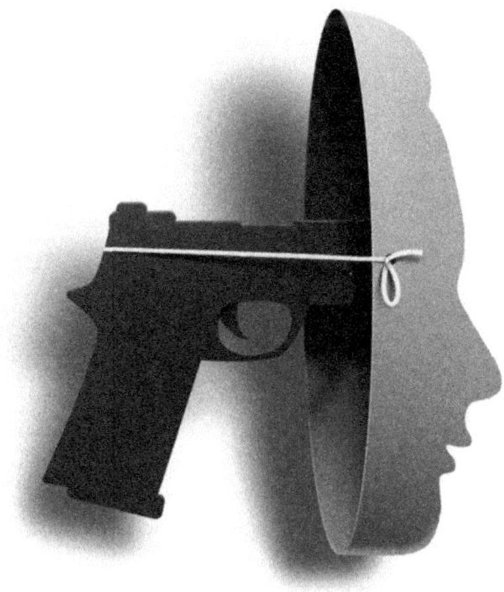

EIKO OJALA

Everytown For Gun Safety, found that in about 11 percent of shootings between January 2009 and July 2015 in which four or more people were killed, concerns about the killer's mental health had been reported to a doctor or other authority before the crime took place.

Under federal law, people who have been involuntarily committed because of mental illness are prohibited from buying guns. The federal government relies on the states to submit records of such commitments to the National Instant Criminal Background Check System, so that would-be gun buyers who have been committed will fail a background check.

In recent years, many more states have made an effort to submit such records to the federal system; the number in the databank has more than doubled since the 2012 mass shooting at a school in Newtown, Conn. After Connecticut began submitting its records in 2007, violent crime among people with disqualifying hospitalizations declined. However, getting state records is still a problem; six states have submitted fewer than 100 records.

A few states have additional prohibitions for those who have been hospitalized but not committed. California, for instance, bars those who have been involuntarily hospitalized for a short time from owning guns for five years, even if they were not committed. For people with severe mental illness who are never hospitalized, tighter gun permitting rules could help. Requiring an in-person application (like getting a driver's license) would make it harder for them to qualify for gun ownership. In the 10 years after Connecticut passed a "permit to purchase" law requiring would-be gun buyers to pass a background check and complete a gun safety course with a certified instructor, gun homicides in the state fell by 40 percent.

In some states, the police may confiscate guns from people at risk of harming themselves or others, some of whom may be mentally ill. Between 1999 and 2009, 11 percent of confiscation warrants in Connecticut, for example, were requested as a result of "mental instability" on the part of the gun owner; by far the largest share, 46 percent, were requested because the owner showed signs of being suicidal.

All of these approaches are worth considering at the state and federal levels as part of a broader effort to reduce gun violence. And, of course, effectively diagnosing and treating mental illness is a worthy goal in itself. But addressing mental health, on its own, will not solve the country's gun violence problem.

CHAPTER 4

The Debate Continues

As society continues to evolve and change, so do issues surrounding gun ownership. Facebook has become involved in efforts to limit gun sales, and major retailers have taken a stand either to not sell guns and ammunition or to restrict open-carry in their stores. Major elections, such as the 2020 presidential election, often include candidates who have strong opinions on gun rights. Experts weigh in on the effect of increased gun rights and the place of mental illness in gun violence.

Global Gun Rights?

COLUMN | BY JOSHUA KURLANTZICK | SEPT. 17, 2006

IN JULY, AS rifle-wielding militias in Iraq slaughtered civilians, the United Nations held a conference on small arms. The conference aimed at creating an international treaty limiting the trade in small arms — weapons designed for personal use, which cause about a thousand deaths worldwide each day. But after intensive debate, and despite the support of many nations, even the normally sunny Kofi Annan had to admit that the conference had collapsed or, as he put it, had "ended without agreeing on an outcome."

One group represented at the conference had reason to celebrate: the National Rifle Association, which in the past decade has been refining its own version of globalization. At first, the group openly fought gun control abroad, but that enabled gun-control advocates to accuse local gun lobbies of selling out to America. In Brazil, the N.R.A. tried a new approach. Brazil has the most gun deaths annually of any country, and last October it held a referendum on a nationwide gun ban. In the run-up to the vote, polls suggested that more than 70 percent of Brazilians supported the ban. Then the Brazilian gun lobby, which previously had emphasized the desirability of gun ownership, began running advertisements that instead suggested that if the government could take away the right to own a weapon (though Brazilians have no constitutional right to bear arms), it could steal other civil liberties. This argument took gun-control advocates by surprise, and on voting day, 64 percent of Brazilians voted against the gun ban. "We gun-control groups failed to anticipate this idea of focusing on rights," admits Denis Mizne of Sou da Paz, a Brazilian public-policy institute. As a report in Foreign Policy revealed, the National Rifle Association lobbyist Charles Cunningham had traveled to Brazil as early as 2003 to impart strategy to local gun advocates, teaching them to emphasize rights instead of weapons.

Around the world, the N.R.A. is finding that a rights-based approach translates into many languages. As the N.R.A.'s executive vice president, Wayne LaPierre, says: "They made the rights argument [in Brazil.] They made the argument that this was being taken away from the people." He pauses. "It caught Iansa" — the International Action Network on Small Arms — "by surprise. They already had the Champagne on ice." In the mid-1990's, the N.R.A. became a nongovernmental observer at the United Nations and helped form a global coalition of pro-gun groups to match disarmament coalitions. At U.N. conferences, this coalition then uses success in national referendums to argue against global treaties. "The vote in Brazil on last Oct. 23 was a mandate," the head of one gun-advocacy group argued at the U.N. conference this July. "The international anti-gun community, especially powerful NGO's, was intimately and extensively involved in supporting the gun-ban referendum. They lost. They did not receive the mandate."

The N.R.A. is in the conservative vanguard: in recent years many conservative groups have been increasingly willing to engage abroad. Going global has several advantages. Organizations get more leverage over U.S. policy: conservative groups' growing knowledge of H.I.V. issues in Africa has given them more say over America's global AIDS policies, leverage that conservatives have used to press abstinence as a leading strategy. Going global also can provide a defense against the influence of international law, which judges like Supreme Court Justice Stephen Breyer have increasingly introduced into American courts. Conservative legal organizations like the Alliance Defense Fund have headed to countries like Sweden to combat international precedent on issues ranging from human cloning to home schooling. And conservatives now realize that by co-opting the language of rights, traditionally employed by the political left, they can export their own ideas of universal rights, whether that means the White House's democratization program or a universal right to bear arms.

JOSHUA KURLANTZICK is special correspondent for The New Republic and a visiting scholar at the Carnegie Endowment for International Peace.

What Bolstering Gun Rights Will Mean

ROOM FOR DEBATE | BY THE NEW YORK TIMES | JUNE 28, 2010

In Room for Debate, The Times invites knowledgeable outside contributors to discuss news events and other timely issues.

THE SUPREME COURT on Monday ruled that the Second Amendment's guarantee of an individual's right to bear arms applied to state and local laws. The case, McDonald v. City of Chicago, involved Chicago's longtime ban on handguns. Justice Samuel Alito, writing for the 5-to-4 majority, said the decision does not imperil every law regulating firearms, like those prohibiting gun possession by felons or bans on firearms in schools. But the court left unanswered just what other types of gun control laws — beyond an outright ban on handguns — might also violate the Second Amendment.

What are the implications of this decision? And how might states and local governments fashion strong policies aimed at stopping gun violence?

Glenn H. Reynolds, law professor, University of Tennessee
James Alan Fox, criminology professor, Northeastern University
John Feinblatt, adviser to Mayor Bloomberg
Jack M. Balkin, Yale Law School
Paul Butler, George Washington Law School

NOW IT'S UP TO THE LOWER COURTS

Glenn Harlan Reynolds is the Beauchamp Brogan Distinguished Professor of Law at the University of Tennessee. He blogs at Instapundit.com and hosts "Instavision" on PJTV.com.

It is not necessary to read (as I am doing) the 214 pages of Supreme Court opinionizing to grasp the key impact of the McDonald opinion: the Second Amendment has now become normal constitutional law.

Even after the Supreme Court's 2008 landmark opinion in District of Columbia v. Heller, it remained possible that the right to arms wouldn't be incorporated against state and local governments. But after McDonald, the Second Amendment joins other provisions of the Bill of Rights that are routinely enforced against both federal and state infringements.

It may wind up being protected fairly well — as, say, First Amendment speech rights generally are — or poorly, as Fourth Amendment rights against search and seizure often are, but it is now a full-fledged part of the Bill of Rights, not a neglected stepchild that has been interpreted out of existence. I view this as something of a vindication, since it was only a few years ago that some commentators were calling talk of the Second Amendment as an individual right crazy, something that only paid shills for the N.R.A. could possibly endorse. That turns out not to be the case.

Most interesting to me about the Thomas opinion in McDonald is its frank recitation of the racist roots of gun control laws, which were intended to disarm blacks, especially after the Civil War and — in the case of New York's Sullivan Law — sometimes recent immigrants as well. Justice Thomas relies heavily on Bob Cottrol and Ray Diamond's pathbreaking article on this subject, which I highly recommend to interested readers.

Of course, as with all Supreme Court opinions, the real action will be in the lower courts, to which fall the grubby tasks of applying the constitutional principles the Supreme Court pronounces. Brannon Denning, a professor at Samford University Law School, and I have been watching this reaction since the Heller opinion, and I look forward to seeing whether those courts embrace the right to arms as willingly as they did with free speech jurisprudence, or as grudgingly as they did with the Supreme Court's commerce clause jurisprudence in the 1990s.

Given the strong similarity between Chicago's ordinance and the one struck down in Heller, it is likely to be overturned below. I will note, however, that as a practical matter, Chicago's gun control law doesn't seem to have worked very well.

CRACKDOWN ON ILLEGAL GUN TRADE

James Alan Fox is the Lipman Family Professor of Criminology, Law and Public Policy at Northeastern University and joined in an amicus brief in McDonald v. Chicago. His blog, Crime & Punishment, deals with criminal behavior and the justice system.

In its decision today, the U.S. Supreme Court has reaffirmed the Second Amendment right of private gun ownership for defending home and family against assailants and intruders. The irony of this ruling is that the now-moribund Chicago handgun ban had, according to statistical evidence presented in an amicus brief submitted to the court, resulted in as many as 1,000 fewer homicides since it was enacted in 1983, especially those occurring in the home and involving family members.

Despite the court's protective stand on gun rights in McDonald and previously in the Heller case, state and local governments still retain the authority — if not responsibility — to defend its citizens from the threat of gun crime through rules of owner licensing and gun registration. Chicago, and other cities, should continue to pursue strategies to regulate and monitor the sale and transfer of firearms for public safety purposes.

Over the past decade, the U.S. Congress has, unfortunately, been decidedly gun-friendly, passing measure after measure that limit law enforcement efforts to disrupt the flow of illegal guns into the hands of criminals.

Such moves as restricting the use of A.T.F. gun tracing data, preventing the A.T.F. from forcing licensed firearms dealers to maintain up-to-date inventories and immunizing the gun industry from civil litigation for shoddy business practices have benefited those who profit by diverting weapons into the illegal gun market. Since 2000, even while homicide rates have declined, gun killings have increased, especially in urban areas; and the percentage of felony-related homicides (those stemming from robbery and other serious offenses) continues to inch upward, now at an all-time high of nearly 75 percent.

Regrettably, the gun debate has polarized the two sides rather than gravitating toward some common ground. Gun control advocates unfairly demonize their rivals with the "gun nut" label. Meanwhile, gun rights supporters worry excessively about the "slippery slope" and allege that their opponents wish to eliminate guns altogether. Of course, most Americans are at neither extreme.

Now that the Supreme Court has spoken, it is time for the middle majority of Americans to speak up in support of sensible gun legislation. They need to urge their lawmakers to stand up to the gun lobby and allow A.T.F. and law enforcement freer rein in their efforts to crack down on the illegal gun trade.

IT'S ALL ABOUT LAW ENFORCEMENT

John Feinblatt is the chief policy adviser to Mayor Michael Bloomberg of New York and the lead architect of the Mayors Against Illegal Guns coalition.

Last year, New York City had fewer murders than any year since 1963. And according to the F.B.I., we are the safest big city in the country. That's because we relentlessly pursue and hold accountable the criminals and traffickers who bring guns to our streets. At the same time, we respect the rights of law-abiding citizens to own guns for protection, collection and sport.

In 2008, the Supreme Court struck down a ban on handguns in District of Columbia v. Heller, while also affirming the constitutionality of reasonable gun ownership restrictions, such as laws that prohibit criminals and the mentally ill from purchasing and obtaining guns. Today's decision mirrors Heller and simply extends its protections to cities and states.

In short, the Supreme Court has ruled that gun ownership is a constitutional right, but like all rights, it is limited. Just as there is no right to yell "Fire!" in a crowded theater, the court has written that there is no right to bring a handgun to a school.

The Supreme Court has struck a balance between the right of individuals to own guns and the responsibility of lawmakers to protect innocent lives. That balance is consistent with New York City's gun laws, which include a permitting process run by the New York Police Department.

We expect the Supreme Court's decision in the Heller and McDonald cases to have little impact on gun trafficking and gun violence. The key to keeping guns out of the hands of criminals (in urban and rural areas) is getting tougher about enforcing existing laws, and closing gaping loopholes that undermine the federal ban on gun purchases by criminals.

That is the focus of Mayors Against Illegal Guns, a bipartisan coalition of 500 mayors from across the country. As polarizing as the debate on guns is in Washington, in the rest of America there is significant consensus on the core issues. A recent poll conducted by Republican pollster Frank Luntz revealed that 83 percent of N.R.A. members believe that "support for Second Amendment rights goes hand-in-hand with keeping illegal guns out of the hands of criminals."

The question that remains is: Will Congress and the White House finally move beyond the ideological debate on gun rights — which the Supreme Court has now settled — and start focusing on tougher, smarter, law enforcement?

CREATING A NATIONAL NORM

Jack M. Balkin is Knight Professor of Constitutional Law and the First Amendment at Yale Law School. He participated in an amicus brief on behalf of petitioners in McDonald v. Chicago.

McDonald v. Chicago raises many arcane legal issues of great interest to constitutional lawyers, but in terms of practical effect, it is more of a pop gun than a big bang. The result was widely expected, and now the case goes back to the lower courts to apply the 2008 decision in District of Columbia v Heller.

Complete bans on the use of handguns in the home for self-defense are likely to be held unconstitutional, as the Heller case suggested. But a wide range of other firearms regulations should be perfectly legal. The Supreme Court signaled as much in Heller and once again in McDonald.

The big difference between applying a constitutional right only against the federal government and applying it against state and local governments is that there are many more state and local regulations of firearms than federal regulations, and these regulations occur in many different varieties.

This increases the number of possible constitutional claims, and it also increases the opportunities for litigation. It does not, however, guarantee that Second Amendment rights will become too robust over time.

We can guess what is likely to happen from the way that courts have protected other federal constitutional rights against states and local governments in the past. Federal judicial protection of fundamental rights tends to converge toward the preferences of the national political coalition, which includes executive branch and law enforcement officials.

Federal courts tend to strike down mostly laws in outlier jurisdictions that are markedly different from the norm. That is what happened in the District of Columbia, and will likely happen in Chicago. More than 40 states already recognize an individual right to bear arms under their own constitutions. By and large, they have upheld most gun control laws under a loose standard of reasonableness. The federal courts will probably follow suit.

Gun control advocates are concerned that a single federal rule for gun rights will leave urban areas defenseless. Ironically, however, a national standard that lumps cities and rural areas together is far more likely to produce moderation than radical change. That is because many more people live in metropolitan than in rural areas, and in the long run their preferences will shape the national political coalition.

PLAYING THE RACE CARD

Paul Butler, a former federal prosecutor, is an associate dean and the Carville Dickinson Benson Research Professor of Law at George Washington University. He is the author of "Let's Get Free: A Hip-Hop Theory of Justice."

Guns don't kill people, the National Rifle Association likes to remind us. People kill people. Likewise, today's Supreme Court decision doesn't kill people, directly. But, as the four dissenting justices noted, the majority's ruling may prove to be "literally destructive." Some Americans are eventually going to die, because this case will lead to the overturning of strict gun control laws that are proven to safe lives.

Justice Alito, who wrote the majority opinion, doesn't necessarily disagree that there may be considerable public safety costs, but he says, blame the Constitution, not me. The problem is the Constitution doesn't say anything directly about what Chicago should do about the problem of too many of its young black citizens shooting each other to death.

You might think that somebody like Justice Alito, who usually favors states' rights, would defer to the local legislature, which in its wisdom passed a law putting tight restrictions on who gets to keep a gun. But the conservative majority has finally found an invocation of federal power it supports. There is something about owning a gun, the court claims, that is as fundamental to our American identity as the right to free speech, or to a jury trial.

One reason that the court's logic looks somewhat disingenuous is how it plays the race card. Justice Alito has finally found, in Otis McDonald, the elderly Chicagoan who brought the case, an African-American claimant for civil rights he supports. He writes at length about how important guns were to protecting the freed slaves from violence by white racists. You'd think Harvard scholar Henry Louis Gates had written this part of the opinion. Or maybe the militant Black Panther Party, which in the 1960s supported the right of every black person to carry a gun while walking down the street, for pretty much the same reasons as the court identifies today.

These are the same five justices who voted to overturn an affirmative action program for the New Haven police department, the same five justices who thought that a voluntary plan to desegregate the Seattle public schools was unconstitutional, the same five justices who rarely do what the N.A.A.C.P. or the Mexican-American Legal Defense Fund ask them to do. It's the same Justice Alito, who during the first

State of the Union message by the first black president, couldn't refrain from mouthing "that's not true" when the president said something with which he disagreed. Now they've all become race men.

It's not every day when four justices of the Supreme Court accuse the other five of having blood on their hands. The majority opinion doesn't immediately lead to any change in a specific law, almost like the court is afraid of what it is setting in motion. But the dissenters were correct. Sooner, rather than later, the blood will flow.

With Move to Limit Gun Sales, Facebook Is Caught in Debate

BY DAVID STREITFELD | MARCH 5, 2014

FACEBOOK WANTS TO unite the world so everyone can talk about everything. One of the big things people want to talk about, it seems, is guns.

The social network is one of the world's largest marketplaces for guns. A DoubleStar AR-15 is offered for $650. A raspberry-colored Taurus pistol can be had for $239.95, a Bushmaster M4 "fresh from the box" for $1,200. "We've got over 550 guns and we need buyers!" posts a Louisiana seller.

Under pressure from law enforcement and advocacy groups, Facebook took steps Wednesday to regulate gun sales on its site as well as on its photo-sharing app Instagram. Pages advertising guns for sale, for instance, will be shielded from minors.

Facebook does not want its growing prominence as a private gun mall to alienate users. Nor does it want to squelch free speech. But if the company hoped its announcement would satisfy everyone and make the issue disappear, the plan backfired.

Gun control groups applauded the changes. So did Michael R. Bloomberg, who is making gun control one of the most visible elements of his career after serving as New York mayor. But the National Rifle Association said the changes were so insignificant that Mr. Bloomberg had "failed."

And Daniel Gross, president of one of the largest gun control groups, the Brady Campaign to Prevent Gun Violence, said little had been achieved.

"I wouldn't even call this a meaningful first step," Mr. Gross said. "There's a simple solution here. Facebook should be prohibiting any post that advertises the unlicensed sale or transfer of firearms in the U.S."

Some large Internet sites have gone further. Craigslist, the informal community website for all sorts of transactions, prohibits the sale of weapons as does the auction site eBay. "We made the unilateral decision to ban all guns in 1999 as part of our commitment to being a responsible online marketplace," Ryan Moore, an eBay spokesman, said Wednesday.

Facebook and Instagram are not e-commerce sites, but with over a billion users they encourage a lot of conversations that establish a framework for offline deals. In some ways, the lack of an actual storefront promotes a willingness to believe there are no rules.

Eric T. Schneiderman, the New York attorney general, sent Mark Zuckerberg, Facebook's chief executive, a letter in November saying that "a recent review of Facebook found a number of groups in which users promoted the sale of assault rifles, handguns, rifles, shotguns and gun parts." He noted that a new New York law requiring background checks could easily be skirted by Facebook users.

Facebook says it strives to be mindful of the needs of all its members.

"Our goal here is to balance people's interest in sharing things that they care about while making sure our community is a safe and responsible one," said Matt Steinfeld, a Facebook spokesman.

The specific changes Facebook is putting in place include deleting posts that seek to circumvent gun laws. It will restrict minors from viewing pages that sell guns. And it will inform potential sellers that private sales could be regulated or prohibited where they live.

But Facebook will be able to take action only when a member of its community alerts it. On Instagram, the process will be a little more automatic. Someone searching for a hashtag like #gunsforsale will get a "content advisory."

Mr. Gross, of the Brady group, said blocking children was the "only tangible thing here." Otherwise, he said, "I don't think Facebook has delivered on what can be done, and what our supporters want to be done."

Facebook's changes came after it had been talking to gun-control groups for as long as a year. Among them are Sandy Hook Promise,

Moms Demand Action for Gun Sense in America, Mr. Bloomberg's Mayors Against Illegal Guns, Americans for Responsible Solutions and the Brady group. Mr. Schneiderman joined the discussion as well.

Mr. Bloomberg said, "We are grateful that Facebook was willing to listen to the Moms, look at the information and adapt its policies to help make sure that people who shouldn't have guns — like minors, felons and other dangerous people — aren't able to get guns via their platform."

There are many competing interests. The group Moms Demand Action received 225,000 signatories to a petition asking Facebook to crack down on illegal gun sales. But the N.R.A. tried to frame its demands as a free-speech issue.

"Bloomberg and the gun-control groups he funds tried to pressure Facebook into shutting down discussion of Second Amendment issues on its social media platforms," Chris W. Cox, executive director of the N.R.A.'s Institute for Legislative Action, said in a statement. "Bloomberg failed."

Siva Vaidhyanathan, a professor of media studies at the University of Virginia who has written often about Internet culture, said Facebook was "entering its adolescence facing all of these moral and political challenges about what to filter and what standards to apply."

He added, "It will need a linguist and a roomful of lawyers to come up with a workable policy to allow some posts about guns to go through and some not to go through."

Already, however, he could see the site taking on more responsibility for what happens on it.

"The moment Facebook gets into the business of blocking what it identifies as gun sales to minors, it is assuming responsibility if something horribly goes wrong," Mr. Vaidhyanathan said.

That almost happened last fall, when a 15-year-old Kentucky boy used Facebook to buy a handgun from an Ohio man. Federal law prohibits the sale of guns across state lines except by licensed dealers, while minors cannot buy handguns in any case.

The youth was arrested with the loaded weapon outside his school's homecoming football game. He said he had bought the gun to be cool. The seller was charged last month with transferring a firearm to an out-of-state resident.

Checking Facts and Falsehoods About Gun Violence and Mental Illness After Parkland Shooting

BY LINDA QIU AND JUSTIN BANK | FEB. 16, 2018

A HEAVILY ARMED young man is accused of killing 17 people after opening fire on terrified students and teachers at Marjory Stoneman Douglas High School in Parkland, Fla., on Wednesday. It was the third mass shooting in the past four months in the United States.

Nikolas Cruz, who has been linked to a history of mental illness, is believed to have used a legally obtained AR-15 in the shooting. The attack has led to widespread conversations about links between gun violence and mental illness, and how lawmakers and interest groups are debating potential policy responses. Below is a look at some facts and falsehoods uttered by Speaker Paul D. Ryan, Republican of Wisconsin; Senator Bernie Sanders, independent of Vermont; and others in the wake of Wednesday's shooting.

"Mental health is often a big problem underlying these tragedies." — House Speaker Paul Ryan

There's a link, but it's more limited than widely thought.

Mr. Ryan's claim reflects a common misconception. According to various polls, roughly half of Americans either believe that failing to identify people with mental health problems is the primary cause of gun violence or that addressing mental health issues would be a major deterrent.

That conclusion is not shared by experts or widely accepted research.

In an analysis of 235 mass killings, many of which were carried out with firearms, 22 percent of the perpetrators could be considered mentally ill.

Overall, mass shootings by people with serious mental illness represent 1 percent of all gun homicides each year, according to the book "Gun Violence and Mental Illness" published by the American Psychiatric Association in 2016.

To be sure, gun violence experts contacted by New York Times reporters have said that barring sales to people who are deemed dangerous by mental health providers could help prevent mass shootings. But the experts said several more measures — including banning assault weapons and barring sales to convicted violent criminals — would be more effective.

And, as The Times has reported, Americans do not appear to have more mental health problems than other developed nations of a comparable size, which experience far fewer mass shootings.

Some further research:

• A 2016 academic study estimated that just 4 percent of violence is associated with serious mental illness alone. "Evidence is clear that the large majority of people with mental disorders do not engage in violence against others, and that most violent behavior is due to factors other than mental illness," the study concluded.

• A 2015 study found that less than 5 percent of gun-related killings in the United States between 2001 and 2010 were committed by people diagnosed with mental illness.

As John T. Monahan, a professor specializing in psychology and law at the University of Virginia, told The Times:

> *"Two things typically happen in the wake of a mass shooting. First, politicians claim that mental illness is the major cause of violence in America. Then, advocates for people with mental illness respond by denying there is any relationship whatsoever between mental illness and violence. Both groups are wrong. Research shows that the association between mental illness and violence is not strong, but it does exist."*

"After 18 school shootings in America in just 43 days of 2018, the Congress might want to consider common-sense gun safety legislation and save innocent lives." — Senator Bernie Sanders

False. There have been 18 instances of weapons being discharged. It would not be fair to call them all shootings.

The figure is drawn from a list maintained by the advocacy group Every Town for Gun Safety. As the group explains on its site, the total includes "any time a firearm discharges a live round inside a school building or on a school campus or grounds."

As The Washington Post, The Washington Examiner and other outlets have pointed out, that includes some incidents that most people would not consider school shootings. For example, the list includes suicides, like a Florida man who shot himself in the parking lot of a school while it was closed. And it also includes accidents like a Minnesota third-grader who pulled the trigger on a police officer's holstered weapon, injuring no one.

"Israel pretty much eliminated [shootings] by placing highly trained people strategically to spot the one common thread — not the weapon, but a person with intent." — Former Gov. Mike Huckabee of Arkansas

This is an interpretation that the Israelis reject.

Israeli officials and experts rejected this version of events after a similar claim was made by Wayne LaPierre, the president of the National Rifle Association, after the 2012 shooting at Sandy Hook Elementary School in Newtown, Conn., in which 20 children and six adults were killed.

"Israel had a whole lot of school shootings until they did one thing. They said, 'We're going to stop it,' and they put armed security in every school, and they have not had a problem since then," Mr. LaPierre said in December 2012 on NBC.

Yigal Palmor, a spokesman for the Israeli Foreign Ministry, told The New York Daily News at the time that the situations in the United States and Israel were "fundamentally different" and said that the measures that Israel enacted were a response to terrorism.

"What removed the danger was not the armed guards, but an overall antiterror policy and antiterror operations, which brought street terrorism down to nearly zero over a number of years," Mr. Palmor said.

"Your very first acts as president, Mr. Trump, was to actually roll back the regulations that were designed to keep firearms out of the hands of the mentally ill." — Late-night host Jimmy Kimmel

True, but the rule's scope was narrow.

After Mr. Trump focused on mental health in his national address on Thursday in response to the Parkland shooting, many journalists, activists and others, like Mr. Kimmel, noted the repeal of a rule that would have prevented "seriously mentally ill" people from purchasing guns.

Federal law already bars anyone who "has been adjudicated as a mental defective or has been committed to any mental institution" from purchasing a gun. And a majority of states have laws requiring them to report mental health information to the national background check system. But gaps in the system still exist.

After the Newtown shooting, President Obama proposed adding another data source to the background check system: reports from the Social Security Administration of people who receive disability benefits through a third party because of mental impairments. According to a 2016 White House fact sheet, the rule would have affected 75,000 people.

It was opposed by the National Rifle Association, but also the American Civil Liberties Union, which said the rule violated civil rights. Some disability rights groups also argued against the rule on the basis that it perpetuated stigmas about mental illness.

Mr. Trump signed a congressional resolution that expressed disapproval of the proposed rule in February 2017, nine months before compliance would have been required.

LINDA QIU is a fact-check reporter, based in Washington. She came to The Times in 2017 from the fact-checking service PolitiFact.

JUSTIN BANK is a senior editor for internet and audience. He was previously a senior editor at The Washington Post.

Justices Won't Hear Case on Waiting Period for Gun Purchases

BY ADAM LIPTAK | FEB. 20, 2018

WASHINGTON — The Supreme Court on Tuesday declined to hear a Second Amendment challenge to a California law that imposes a 10-day waiting period on firearms purchases.

As is their custom, the justices gave no reasons for deciding not to hear the case. The court has turned away many Second Amendment cases in recent years, to the frustration of gun-rights groups and some conservative justices.

Justice Clarence Thomas filed an impassioned 14-page dissent in the case, Silvester v. Becerra, No. 17-342. "As evidenced by our continued inaction in this area," he wrote, "the Second Amendment is a disfavored right in this court."

In 2008, in District of Columbia v. Heller, the Supreme Court ruled that the Second Amendment protects an individual right to keep guns at home for self-defense.

Since then, the court has said little about what other laws may violate the Second Amendment. In the lower courts, few challenges to gun control laws since the Heller decision have succeeded.

The California law at issue in the new case was upheld by the United States Court of Appeals for the Ninth Circuit, in San Francisco, which accepted the state's arguments that the waiting period was justified by the need to conduct background checks and the desirability of a "cooling off" period for gun buyers inclined to commit immediate violence.

Justice Thomas wrote that many background checks can be completed quickly and that the cooling off period made no sense for people who already owned a gun. "Common sense suggests that subsequent purchasers contemplating violence or self-harm would use the gun they already own, instead of taking all the steps to legally buy a new one in California," he wrote.

He said the appeals court's decision was one of many in which Second Amendment rights have not been taken seriously in the lower courts.

"The Ninth Circuit's deviation from ordinary principles of law is unfortunate, though not surprising," Justice Thomas wrote. "Its dismissive treatment of petitioners' challenge is emblematic of a larger trend."

"Our continued refusal to hear Second Amendment cases only enables this kind of defiance," he wrote. "We have not heard argument in a Second Amendment case for nearly eight years."

Justice Thomas wrote that the Supreme Court has been much more attentive to other constitutional rights and would surely have mustered the four votes needed to put a case on the court's docket had a different right been at issue.

"I suspect that four members of this court would vote to review a 10-day waiting period for abortions, notwithstanding a state's purported interest in creating a 'cooling off' period," he wrote. "I also suspect that four members of this court would vote to review a 10-day waiting period on the publication of racist speech, notwithstanding a state's purported interest in giving the speaker time to calm down."

"The right to keep and bear arms is apparently this court's constitutional orphan," Justice Thomas wrote. "And the lower courts seem to have gotten the message."

Why Doesn't America Know More About Gun Safety?

EDITORIAL | BY THE NEW YORK TIMES | AUG. 7, 2019

Congress can resolve an enduring problem: the lack of federal funding for research on guns.

The editorial board represents the opinions of the board, its editor and the publisher. It is separate from the newsroom and the Op-Ed section.

IN THE WAKE of yet another spate of mass shootings, America is confronted with many questions. Among them: Do waiting periods on gun purchases curb gun violence or reduce the number of gun-related deaths and injuries? What about gun buybacks? Or age restrictions? Public health experts know that far more people die of gunshot wounds than of cholera or diphtheria or polio — but they know far less about how to prevent gun violence than they do those other causes of death. Because when it comes to guns, research is still maddeningly limited.

For the first time in two decades, members of Congress have taken a concrete step toward changing that. In June, the House passed a bill earmarking federal money for research into gun violence and safety. If the bill clears the Senate, and the president signs it into law, the proposed allotment — $50 million split evenly between the National Institutes of Health and the Centers for Disease Control and Prevention — would help scientists answer some crucial questions about the nation's enduring gun violence problem and how best to solve it.

It's no mystery why such research has lagged. In 1996 Congress eliminated most federal funding for gun safety research and passed a provision known as the Dickey Amendment that prohibited the use of federal money for anything that could be construed as gun control advocacy. Those measures — which followed concerted lobbying by the National Rifle Association — had such a chilling effect on research into gun safety that even the amendment's author, Jay Dickey, an

Arkansas Republican who died in 2017, came to regret it: Federal agencies were discouraged from even gathering data that might suggest the need for stricter gun laws. And researchers were scared away from a field that was desperate for intelligent inquiry, but mired in politics and starved of federal support.

Since the amendment was enacted, more than 600,000 people have been shot in the United States and tens of thousands have died.

It remains to be seen whether the House provision will go the way of most gun-related legislation: felled by the first Republican-controlled entity it encounters — in this case, the Senate. But the recent shootings in El Paso, Tex.; Dayton, Ohio; and Gilroy, Calif., with 34 deaths and dozens of injuries between them, have once again put pressure on lawmakers from both sides of the aisle to do something.

There is much that we do already know about guns. Experts tend to agree, for example, that prohibiting violent criminals from buying guns and expanding background checks would go a long way toward curbing gun violence. It's also clear that states in which guns are more tightly regulated have fewer gun-related deaths than those with laxer gun laws; guns tend to make a home less safe, not more so; and more robust gun regulation can curb the suicide rate. (The vast majority of gun-related deaths in the United States are from suicide.)

But it would be helpful if policymakers and the public had more data on which policies and procedures reduce gun-related deaths, which factors contribute most heavily to gun violence and what motivates people to buy guns in the first place. Also needed: reliable, comprehensive data on the number of guns in circulation and the people who own them.

In recent years, private foundations and state legislatures have tried to fill the gap left by congressional neglect, devoting millions of dollars to research on gun violence and gun safety. These efforts have succeeded in building the infrastructure and developing the human resources needed to sustain a major research effort. But only a large-scale, federally funded initiative can tackle the scope of questions that need answers and produce the kind of evidence required to inform effective policy.

Congress now has a real chance to create just such a program. Senators would do well to support the House appropriation — or, even better, expand on it. If they did, scientists and policymakers might finally be able to treat gun safety like the public health problem that it so clearly is.

On Gun Control, 2020 Democrats Agree: No Reason to Hold Back

BY REID J. EPSTEIN AND THOMAS KAPLAN | AUG. 12, 2019

DES MOINES — Democrats running for president have engaged in bitter disputes this year over topics like health care, immigration and criminal justice.

But after mass shootings in El Paso and Dayton, Ohio, jolted the nation earlier this month, the field of 2020 contenders seemed to move in lock step toward more aggressive gun control positions without resistance from the party's moderate voices.

The result is that an issue currently at the top of voters' minds is producing little disagreement between the centrist and liberal Democrats seeking the White House. Instead, a contest has emerged over who can deliver the most effective pitch for new gun control measures, with the proper emotional punch.

"On policy, people aren't that far apart," Senator Amy Klobuchar of Minnesota said in an interview aboard the Sky Glider gondola at the Iowa State Fair. "I think the difference is who can actually get this done."

Democrats are used to arguing over health care, a debate that has been central to the party's identity for decades. But there hasn't been a robust policy discussion on gun control in a presidential primary since 2000, when Vice President Al Gore and former Senator Bill Bradley of New Jersey debated the wisdom of a national gun licensing system.

Now, candidates are navigating a Democratic electorate driven in part by young voters who came of age in the mass shooting era and who have little tolerance for kowtowing to a long-held view that gun rights are sacrosanct. The idea of a gun licensing system has returned to the center of the discussion, backed by candidates like Senator Cory

CHRISTOPHER LEE FOR THE NEW YORK TIMES

From left, Alanna Miller, Neuteyshe Felizor and Sari Kaufman, who survived the Parkland shooting, listened to Democratic presidential candidates speak at the Everytown for Gun Safety forum in Des Moines on Saturday.

Booker of New Jersey, and many candidates have vowed to reinstate a ban on assault-style weapons.

The more modest playbook of recent years — calling for universal background checks on gun purchasers and more federal funding for research into gun violence — no longer satisfies Democrats, even though both proposals are anathema to Republicans aligned with the National Rifle Association.

"Democrats running for president, I think, have got to be bolder than what they are on this gun issue," former Senator Tom Harkin of Iowa said Sunday after appearing at an event in West Des Moines with Senator Kirsten Gillibrand of New York.

In the health care debate, candidates from the party's centrist wing have warned of scaring off voters with ambitious plans like "Medicare for all." But there is no Democrat in the race warning that aggressive gun control proposals go too far.

Asked if it was possible for the party's nominee to go too far on gun control, Ms. Gillibrand replied: "No. I think the American people are behind us."

Nowhere was the power of the movement — and new financing behind it — more evident than Saturday in Des Moines, where 16 presidential candidates appeared at a gun violence forum organized in less than a week by Everytown for Gun Safety, the gun control organization financed primarily by Michael R. Bloomberg, the former New York City mayor.

"I have to tell you, it says a lot about how much you've accomplished that so many presidential candidates are here today," Mr. Bloomberg told a crowd of local activists and gun violence survivors who were bused and flown in for the event. "The big reason for the historic unity in the Democratic Party on guns, and the reason this historic gathering has come together, is that we built a grass-roots army with six million supporters."

Senator Elizabeth Warren of Massachusetts used the Everytown forum to roll out a plan that set a goal of reducing gun deaths by 80 percent and called for a gun licensing program. On Sunday, former Representative Beto O'Rourke of Texas also came out for gun licensing, as have several other candidates.

And former Vice President Joseph R. Biden Jr., in an opinion piece published this week in The New York Times, said he wanted to reinstate the ban on assault-style weapons he championed in 1994. (The prohibition expired when Republicans who controlled Congress in 2004 declined to renew it.)

Mr. Booker, who unveiled a gun control plan in May, said in an interview that calling only for background checks and a ban on assault-style weapons was not sufficient to solve the nation's gun violence problem.

"We need to shift the terms of this debate and make solutions bolder, more evidence-based and shift what people think of as common sense," Mr. Booker said.

CHRISTOPHER LEE FOR THE NEW YORK TIMES

Senator Amy Klobuchar of Minnesota was among the 16 Democratic candidates who spoke at the forum, organized by Everytown for Gun Safety.

Despite Mr. Booker's push, Democrats interviewed at the Everytown forum and elsewhere in Iowa this weekend struggled to identify significant differences among the candidates' approaches to gun control.

"They pretty much all had the same message," said Anne Suchomel, 71, who traveled from southeast Minnesota to attend the forum in Des Moines.

At the state fair pork chop line, Scott Kirkpatrick, a retired golf professional from nearby Windsor Heights, Iowa, said he failed to see "much difference between any of them on guns."

In Iowa's rural precincts, Democratic officials warned that talk of licensing and bans on types of weapons were likely to repel voters in places where gun ownership rates are higher than in urban Des Moines.

"One big hurdle for our nominee will be to overcome the stereotype that Democrats want to take away everyone's guns," said Catherine Crooks, the Democratic Party chairwoman in Franklin County, population 10,124. "That isn't the goal, the goal is responsible gun ownership. It needs to be made quite clear."

Instead of articulating differences on gun control, the candidates are aiming to demonstrate their commitment to the issue through emotional displays.

Gov. Steve Bullock of Montana speaks about losing his 11-year-old nephew to a 1994 school shooting in Butte, Mont. Ms. Gillibrand describes her conversion from an N.R.A.-backed member of Congress to a gun control proponent by talking about meeting with mothers of gun violence victims in Brooklyn after her 2009 appointment to the Senate.

And at the annual Wing Ding dinner Friday night in Clear Lake, Iowa, Representative Tim Ryan of Ohio, who is currently an afterthought in polls, brought the crowd to its feet by recounting a bus trip he took last week to Kentucky, where he protested Senator Mitch McConnell's refusal to hold a vote on legislation that would expand background checks.

"We took the fight to his backyard, telling him that we need gun reform in the United States of America and we need it now. We need it now," Mr. Ryan said. "People are dying on the streets of this country, getting killed by weapons that were made for battlefields, not neighborhoods and places like Dayton, Ohio."

Former Gov. John Hickenlooper of Colorado, who enacted expanded background checks and limits on the size of ammunition magazines in his state after a 2012 shooting that killed 12 at a movie theater in Aurora, Colo., said the N.R.A. would caricature whoever wins the nomination as a gun-grabber, so Democrats may as well offer an assertive platform.

Mr. Hickenlooper is familiar with the N.R.A.'s influence: It backed a successful recall campaign in 2013 to remove from office two Democratic state senators who voted for the new laws.

"Whoever the Democrat is, the N.R.A. is going to go full hog to beat them," Mr. Hickenlooper said. "The N.R.A. is first and foremost a

JORDAN GALE FOR THE NEW YORK TIMES

Senator Cory Booker of New Jersey unveiled a gun control plan in May.

trade association, and their members need to sell more guns. They're going to push as much money as they can raise against whoever the Democratic candidate is."

Democrats here said the mass shootings in El Paso and Dayton left them focused on finding a candidate who would enact gun control measures — and concerned for their own safety.

Anthony Atlas, 33, who works for an agriculture technology company in Iowa City, brought his 6-month-old son, Orin, to the state fair Saturday. For the first time, he said, he worried about what would happen if a shooting took place at the fairgrounds.

"I was concerned about going to the state fair," he said. "That's a weird thing to worry about."

THOMAS KAPLAN is a political reporter based in Washington. He previously covered Congress, the 2016 presidential campaign and New York state government.

More Retail Chains Ask Customers Not to Carry Guns Openly

BY KAREN ZRAICK | SEPT. 6, 2019

CVS, Walgreens and Wegmans joined Walmart and Kroger in asking customers not to openly carry firearms.

SEVERAL MORE OF the country's most ubiquitous retail chains said this week that they will ask customers to refrain from openly carrying guns in their stores. The requests, days after Walmart announced a similar policy, marked a notable shift in the debate about the presence of guns in everyday life in the United States.

In a short statement posted Thursday, CVS Health requested that customers, other than authorized law enforcement personnel, do not bring firearms into its 9,900 stores in the country. Walgreens, with 9,500 stores, did so as well. Both chains noted that they were joining other retailers. Wegmans, a supermarket chain with 99 stores mainly in the Northeast, noted its request on Twitter.

"The sight of someone with a gun can be alarming, and we don't want anyone to feel that way at Wegmans," the tweet said.

As private entities, the retailers have the right to restrict guns in their stores. But it remained unclear how they might compel customers to comply, and the policies were framed as requests, not outright bans. Several other large chains have enacted similarly worded policies over the last several years, including Starbucks, Target, Costco and Chipotle.

The most recent wave of announcements began on Tuesday, when Walmart, the nation's largest retailer with more than 4,000 stores, said it would stop selling ammunition that can be used in military-style rifles as well as all handgun ammunition, and it would discourage customers from openly carrying guns, even in states where it is legal to do so.

"We will treat law-abiding customers with respect, and we will have a very nonconfrontational approach," Walmart's chief executive, Doug McMillon, said in a statement.

Shortly after Walmart's announcement, Kroger, which is headquartered in Cincinnati and operates more than 2,700 supermarkets, said it too was requesting that its customers not carry weapons into its stores.

In the statement, Jessica Adelman, vice president of corporate affairs, noted that Kroger had completely exited the firearm and ammunition business a year ago.

"Kroger has demonstrated with our actions that we recognize the growing chorus of Americans who are no longer comfortable with the status quo and who are advocating for concrete and common sense gun reforms," she said.

She said the company would also push lawmakers to strengthen background checks and to "remove weapons from those who have been found to pose a risk for violence."

In his statement, Mr. McMillon said that Walmart decided to change its policy in the wake of the Aug. 3 shooting at a Walmart in El Paso, which left 22 people dead.

He noted that after the shooting, there were several episodes "where individuals attempting to make a statement and test our response have entered our stores carrying weapons in a way that frightened or concerned our associates and customers."

He added that even some well-intentioned customers had inadvertently caused alarm, triggering evacuations and law enforcement mobilizations.

"We believe the opportunity for someone to misinterpret a situation, even in open-carry states, could lead to tragic results," Mr. McMillon said.

The Walmart statement noted that there was no change in regard to concealed-carry by customers with permits, and said that new signs would be posted about the policy in the coming weeks.

Gun laws vary widely, but more than 40 states allow some form of open-carry, according to the Giffords Law Center to Prevent Gun Violence, a gun control advocacy group. Some states require special permits or for the weapon to be unloaded, or restrict open-carry policies in cities. There are often exceptions to open-carry laws in schools, public facilities or places where alcohol is served.

Shannon Watts, the founder of the gun-control group Moms Demand Action for Gun Sense in America, called open-carry "a dangerous and culturally reprehensible practice" and applauded the companies for taking action.

"Ultimately this is about getting companies to protect their customers when lawmakers aren't protecting their constituents," she said in a phone interview.

Ms. Watts urged legislators to take action as they return to Washington. Walmart's statement also called on Congress to increase background checks and consider a new assault weapon ban.

The National Rifle Association strongly criticized Walmart's statement, saying it was "shameful to see Walmart succumb to the pressure of the anti-gun elites."

"Lines at Walmart will soon be replaced by lines at other retailers who are more supportive of America's fundamental freedoms," the organization predicted in a statement on Tuesday.

The N.R.A. on Friday directed a reporter to Tuesday's statement.

KAREN ZRAICK is a breaking news and general assignment reporter who writes frequently about gender. She has also worked as an editor on the International desk and in news curation.

Pelosi and Schumer, in Push for Gun Safety Legislation, Urge Trump to Defy N.R.A.

BY SHERYL GAY STOLBERG | SEPT. 9, 2019

WASHINGTON — The top two Democrats in Congress called on Sunday for President Trump to defy the National Rifle Association and get behind legislation, already passed by the House but blocked in the Senate, to expand background checks to nearly all gun buyers.

With gun control high on Congress's agenda as lawmakers return to Washington this week after their August recess, Speaker Nancy Pelosi and Senator Chuck Schumer, the Democratic leader, sent a joint letter to the president, telling him that his "urgent, personal intervention is needed to stem the endless massacres of our fellow Americans by gunfire" and that he had a "historic opportunity to save lives."

The letter, which Ms. Pelosi and Mr. Schumer intend to follow with a news conference on Monday, is part of what Democrats say will be an all-out push for gun safety legislation this fall. In it, they asked Mr. Trump to express his support for H.R. 8, the bill passed by the House that requires background checks for private gun sales, including those at gun shows and over the internet. Senator Mitch McConnell, the Republican leader, has so far refused to take up the measure, which is strongly opposed by the N.R.A.

"We implore you to seize this moment when your leadership and influence over Republicans in Congress on the issue of guns is so critical," they wrote in the letter, which was obtained by The New York Times. "Please do not squander it by acceding to N.R.A.-backed proposals or other weak ideas that will do nothing to stop the continuing, horrific spread of gun violence and may, in some cases, actually make our communities less safe."

ANNA MONEYMAKER/THE NEW YORK TIMES

Senator Chuck Schumer, the Democratic leader, and Speaker Nancy Pelosi wrote that President Trump had a "historic opportunity to save lives."

The letter is an effort to put Mr. Trump and Mr. McConnell into a box on gun control legislation — and, perhaps, to ensure that Republicans and the president take the blame if nothing gets signed into law. The president initially expressed support in early August for "very meaningful background checks" after a pair of deadly mass shootings in Texas and Ohio but stopped short of endorsing the bill passed by the House. His stance, however, appeared to have softened — as has been the case with Mr. Trump in the past — after talks with gun rights advocates.

Mr. McConnell has said he expected the Senate to debate gun control sometime after lawmakers returned to Washington on Monday. But he has also said repeatedly that he would not put legislation on the floor for a vote unless Mr. Trump was willing to sign it — a point that another member of the Republican leadership, Senator Roy Blunt of Missouri, echoed on Sunday.

"We are not going to vote on bills on the Senate floor that the president is not willing to sign," Mr. Blunt said on NBC's "Meet the Press." "The president needs to step up here and set some guidelines for what he would do."

The letter comes as the debate over gun control — one of the most contentious and intractable issues in American politics — is changing rapidly in Washington. So far this year in the United States, firearms have been involved in at least 38 mass killings, which the Justice Department defines as three or more fatalities in a single episode, excluding the gunman. In August alone, 53 people in the United States died in mass killings by firearms.

The shift is evident in Congress and also on the presidential campaign trail; gone are the days when Democrats like John Kerry, the 2004 presidential nominee, felt compelled to have themselves photographed going hunting. (The White House issued such a photograph of President Barack Obama in 2013.) Today's Democratic candidates are falling over one another to see who can issue the most aggressive gun safety platforms.

Yet some Republicans, especially in states where there have been mass shootings, are also calling for gun safety legislation. In Texas, where there were multiple deadly shootings in August, Lt. Gov. Dan Patrick, a staunch proponent of gun rights, called on Friday for background checks on private gun sales.

In Washington, the August shootings prompted Republicans to quickly rally around another type of gun control legislation: so-called red flag laws, which make it easier for law enforcement to take guns away from people deemed dangerous by a judge. In the Senate, Lindsey Graham, Republican of South Carolina, and Richard Blumenthal, Democrat of Connecticut, are sponsoring a red flag bill.

The massacres also revived talk of the bipartisan background checks bill known as the Manchin-Toomey bill, after its Senate sponsors, Joe Manchin III, Democrat of West Virginia, and Patrick J. Toomey, Republican of Pennsylvania. But the legislation, which includes exemptions for gun transfers for family members and friends, is not as expansive as the House bill, and many Republicans remain uncomfortable with it. It fell to a Senate filibuster in 2013.

At the direction of Mr. Trump, top White House officials have been engaged in bipartisan talks with lawmakers, including Mr. Manchin and Mr. Toomey, about what kind of gun legislation the president might be willing to support — and what Democrats would agree to.

An administration official participating in the talks, who spoke on the condition of anonymity because he was not authorized to disclose internal deliberations, said after a recent deadly shooting spree in West Texas that they were making "a lot of progress in good faith," but had reached no agreement. On Sunday, the official said the status of the talks was unchanged.

Mr. McConnell, meanwhile, has directed three top committee chairmen in the Senate — Mr. Graham of the Judiciary Committee, Lamar Alexander of the health committee and Roger Wicker of the commerce committee — to engage in "bipartisan discussions of potential solutions to help protect our communities without infringing on Americans' constitutional rights."

Passing gun legislation has long been one of the most intractable issues in Washington. Democrats typically talk about gun restrictions — many are now calling for an assault weapons ban, which stands virtually no chance of passing the Senate — while Republicans typically talk about the issue of mental health in relation to gun control.

During his "Meet the Press" interview on Sunday, Mr. Blunt expressed concern that the current debate would end in a stalemate, just as it did after the 2012 massacre at Sandy Hook Elementary School in Newtown, Conn.

"I'm afraid what's going to happen here is what always happens — is we take this silly, 'If we don't get everything, we won't do anything,' " he said, "and fail to do the things we could do, with more early mental health help."

Beto O'Rourke Urges Banks to Cut Services for Gun Sales

BY JACEY FORTIN | SEPT. 12, 2019

The candidate said he wanted credit card companies and other financial institutions to stop providing services for sales of assault-style weapons, among other measures.

BETO O'ROURKE, THE Democratic presidential candidate, on Thursday called on banks and credit card companies to address gun violence by refusing to provide services for some firearms sales.

In a statement, Mr. O'Rourke's campaign said he wanted the financial institutions to stop providing services for sales of assault-style weapons — or any firearms that are sold without background checks — and to stop doing business with manufacturers that produce assault-style weapons.

"However inadvertent or deliberate, credit card companies and banks profit off of those who terrorize our communities," Mr. O'Rourke said in an email to voters on Thursday. "And we know that in this moment, no one can sit on the sidelines. Everyone has a responsibility to do their part."

The statement came on the same day of a concerted effort by business leaders to influence the gun debate. In a letter on Thursday, the heads of 145 companies in the United States — including Twitter, Uber, Levi Strauss, Amalgamated Bank and Dick's Sporting Goods — urged Senate leaders to consider an expansion of background checks and stronger "red flag" laws.

Mr. O'Rourke's plan was informed by a New York Times investigation last year that reviewed police reports, bank records and investigator notes from a decade of mass shootings and found that many of the killers had used credit to stockpile high-powered weapons.

In response to that reporting, some banks and credit card networks said that customers were entitled to privacy and independence, and

JOHN TULLY FOR THE NEW YORK TIMES

"However inadvertent or deliberate, credit card companies and banks profit off of those who terrorize our communities," Beto O'Rourke said in an email to voters on Thursday.

that it was not the companies' responsibility to create systems to track gun purchases that would allow them to report suspicious patterns.

Several bank and credit card companies did not respond to requests for comment on Thursday. Visa did not comment on Mr. O'Rourke's proposal, but said in a statement that it agreed with the 145 companies that had called on Congress to advance gun control legislation such as expanding background checks and implementing "red flag" laws.

Some banks have revised their policies in recent years. Citigroup said in March 2018 that it would work only with clients that agreed to certain restrictions on firearm sales, and Bank of America said in April 2018 that it would stop lending money to gun manufacturers that make military-inspired firearms for civilian use.

Payment systems including PayPal, Square and Apple Pay have rules banning firearm sales using their systems.

Mr. O'Rourke, a former Texas representative in Congress who embarked on an unsuccessful but profile-raising Senate run last year, used to represent his hometown, El Paso, where a mass shooting at a Walmart killed 22 people on Aug. 3.

The next day, nine people were killed in another shooting in Dayton, Ohio.

Mr. O'Rourke had an angry, impassioned response to the violence and spent the week off the campaign trail as many of his competitors traveled to Iowa for the state fair and other party activities. The episode drew new attention to Mr. O'Rourke's flagging campaign, although he still lags in the national polls. He has made gun control a central issue in his presidential bid.

Some companies have waded into the gun control debate this year. Walmart said this month that it would stop selling ammunition that can be used in military-style rifles, discourage its customers from openly carrying guns in its stores, and call on Congress to increase background checks and consider a ban on assault-style rifles. Other retailers, including Kroger, CVS, Walgreens and the Wegmans grocery chain, have asked customers to refrain from openly carrying guns in their stores.

Mr. O'Rourke released an aggressive plan to combat gun violence last month, shortly after he recast his campaign as less of a traditional travel itinerary and more of a moral crusade against President Trump.

The plan would require universal background checks for gun purchases; create a national gun registry; limit the influence of the National Rifle Association by banning political action committee contributions to members of Congress; and ban assault-style weapons, silencers, bump stocks and high-capacity magazines.

The plan would also institute a national firearm buyback program, which would be mandatory for assault-style weapons, under penalty of fine, and would be voluntary for handguns.

As Trump Weighs Gun Safety Bills, Barr's Plan Draws Skepticism

BY SHERYL GAY STOLBERG | SEPT. 18, 2019

Attorney General William P. Barr has floated a plan to expand background checks for gun buyers, but President Trump has yet to give it his blessing.

WASHINGTON — As President Trump weighs potential gun safety legislation, his attorney general on Wednesday floated a plan to expand background checks for gun buyers, but the idea was met with skepticism from key Republicans and appeared to face serious obstacles on Capitol Hill.

The proposal being circulated by Attorney General William P. Barr is similar to the so-called Manchin-Toomey bill, which would extend the current background checks system to all commercial gun sales, including those at gun shows and online. That bill fell to a Senate filibuster in 2013.

The White House made clear that the Barr proposal — which senators described as an "ideas list" or a work in progress — has not yet received Mr. Trump's blessing, further underscoring the degree to which bipartisan talks around gun safety could fail. Mr. Barr, speaking to reporters in the Capitol, also played it down, saying he was "just kicking around some ideas" to see what could gain traction in the Senate.

Mr. Trump, for his part, took to Twitter on Wednesday in what appeared to be a proactive effort to lay blame on Democrats should the bipartisan talks fail. He singled out Beto O'Rourke of Texas, a former congressman and current 2020 Democratic presidential candidate, who has proposed a mandatory government program to buy back assault weapons — an idea that makes even some Democrats skittish.

"Dummy Beto made it much harder to make a deal," Mr. Trump tweeted. "Convinced many that Dems just want to take your guns away. Will continue forward!"

On Wednesday evening, Mr. Barr sat down with three of the Senate's strongest advocates of expanded background checks: Senators Christopher S. Murphy, Democrat of Connecticut, and the sponsors of the Manchin-Toomey bill, Joe Manchin III, Democrat of West Virginia, and Patrick J. Toomey, Republican of Pennsylvania.

"There's no question, the heart of the attorney general's idea is a mechanism for expanding background checks beyond what we have today," Mr. Toomey said, adding, "I have colleagues who are open to that so I'm modestly encouraged."

Mr. Manchin also sounded upbeat: "I personally think the president wants to do something. We would not be this engaged for this long a period of time if he didn't."

Mr. Murphy, though, was cautious: "Just finished meeting w Attorney General Barr w @SenToomey and @Sen_JoeManchin," he wrote on Twitter. "It was a really good discussion. But the fact remains that there is no good deal that the gun lobby will support. Now, the White House has a choice to make."

But Republicans who favor gun rights said they wanted more specifics, and several said it was pointless to even talk about Mr. Barr's plan at this point. As the nation's chief law enforcement officer, the attorney general will be a central figure in the debate over gun legislation, but senators agree that the president will have the final say.

"My question was: 'Where is the president on this?' And I asked this question directly: 'Is this something the president supports?' And they didn't have an answer for that," said Senator Josh Hawley, Republican of Missouri, who met with Mr. Barr on Tuesday evening. "That's an important piece. If the president doesn't support it, then there's no point."

And Senator Ted Cruz, Republican of Texas, who also met with Mr. Barr on Tuesday evening, warned against any legislation that "raised the specter of confiscation" and said he was not interested in a bill that would "restrict the Second Amendment rights of law-abiding citizens."

Mr. Cruz is pushing an alternative bill — the so-called lie and try measure, which would make it easier for law enforcement to prosecute people who lie on background checks. That idea is also included in the proposal that Mr. Barr has circulated.

The issue of gun violence has burst onto the Washington agenda after a string of mass shootings that terrorized the nation over the summer. Democrats have been demanding that the president embrace a House-passed bill expanding background checks to cover even private gun sales. But that idea is a nonstarter in a Senate controlled by Republicans, as even Mr. Murphy concedes.

"I wish they would endorse H.R. 8, but that's not going to happen," he said, referring to the House bill, adding, "so this is an iterative process."

Unlike the House bill, the Manchin-Toomey bill would cover only commercial sales, meaning that sales between friends and family members would be exempted. Only two Republicans who voted in favor of it in 2013 — Mr. Toomey and Senator Susan Collins of Maine — remain in the Senate.

And while some Republican newcomers, notably Senator Mitt Romney of Utah, have said they are inclined to support it, the measure draws opposition from many, like Mr. Hawley, who are concerned that it would lead to a federal registry of gun owners, which gun rights advocates strongly oppose.

The proposal being circulated by Mr. Barr, first reported by The Daily Caller, calls for a "newly created class of licensed transfer agents" who would not sell guns, but would be authorized by the government to conduct background checks. Mr. Toomey described it as "a different mechanism" from the Manchin-Toomey bill.

SHERYL GAY STOLBERG is a congressional correspondent. In 21 years at The Times, she has been a science correspondent, national correspondent, political features reporter and White House correspondent.

Trump on Virginia Gun Dispute: 2nd Amendment 'Under Very Serious Attack'

BY TIMOTHY WILLIAMS | JAN. 18, 2020

The president weighed in before thousands were expected to gather in Virginia's capital for a gun rights rally.

RICHMOND, VA. — Days before a planned gun rights rally that has set Virginia's capital on edge, President Trump warned that state Democrats were threatening Americans' right to bear arms.

"Your 2nd Amendment is under very serious attack in the Great Commonwealth of Virginia," Mr. Trump wrote on Twitter on Friday. "That's what happens when you vote for Democrats, they will take your guns away. Republicans will win Virginia in 2020. Thank you Dems!"

The state legislature, where Democrats recently took control for the first time in a generation, is considering several gun control bills, including measures that would require background checks for people purchasing firearms and give municipalities the authority to ban weapons in public buildings.

Thousands of people are expected to descend on the Capitol in Richmond on Monday to protest those measures, in a state where hunting is popular and gun ownership is common in rural areas. Several men with ties to right-wing militias who had planned to attend the rally have been arrested in recent days.

On Saturday, the area around the State Capitol was enclosed by a temporary chain-link fence, barricades and patrolled by groups of law enforcement officers.

Gov. Ralph Northam declared a state of emergency and banned firearms and other weapons on the Capitol grounds this week, further inflaming gun rights activists. The order was challenged in court by the rally's organizers, the Virginia Citizens Defense League. On Friday evening, the State Supreme Court upheld the ban.

Mr. Trump's position on gun rights has been difficult to pin down during his time in office. He supported "meaningful background checks" in the weeks after deadly mass shootings in Texas and Ohio last year, but later walked back that support after meeting with gun rights activists, including the president of the National Rifle Association.

That turnabout mirrored the president's shift after the 2018 shooting in Parkland, Fla., when he expressed support for stronger gun controls and then backtracked after speaking with N.R.A. officials.

In Virginia, Mr. Northam released a statement on Friday saying that the vast majority of those planning to attend the rally on Monday had no interest in creating disturbances, but that some were bent on stoking violence.

"Over the past few days, the news has confirmed that this rally is attracting extreme individuals and groups — including national hate, neo-Nazi, and white supremacist groups — who are threatening violence and looking to advance a violent agenda."

Amid Tight Security, Virginia Gun Rally Draws Thousands of Supporters

BY TIMOTHY WILLIAMS, SABRINA TAVERNISE, ZOLAN KANNO-YOUNGS AND SARAH MERVOSH

PUBLISHED JAN. 20, 2020 | UPDATED JAN. 22, 2020

Some 22,000 people, many of them armed, flooded the streets around the State Capitol to protest gun control proposals from the new Democratic majority.

RICHMOND, VA. — Some people streamed in on buses from faraway cities. Others drove cars through the night from places like Indianapolis and Fredericksburg, Texas, logging hundreds of miles and leaning on coffee and Red Bull. Still others came from only a few counties over, but carrying the same vehement message as the rest: Leave gun laws alone.

Thousands of people descended on Richmond, the capital of Virginia, on Monday to show support for the rights of gun owners as a push for gun control measures by that state's newly empowered Democrats has inserted Virginia into a nationwide debate over gun violence and the Second Amendment.

"I don't like what they are doing to our rights," said Raymond Pfaff, 85, from Louisa County, Va., who wore a yellow sign around his neck that read, "First Gun Control and Then People Control."

"Guns protected this country for a couple of hundred years, and this two-faced governor just wants to take them," he said, referring to Gov. Ralph Northam, a Democrat who has agreed to sign provisions banning guns in parks and limiting handgun purchases if Virginia lawmakers approve them.

"I'm a patriotic American," Mr. Pfaff said. "The left is going so far left right now."

Virginia has a long history of supporting gun rights. Only last year, after a mass shooting in Virginia Beach that left 12 people dead, a special lawmaking session on gun control ended in 90 minutes without any action.

VICTOR J. BLUE FOR THE NEW YORK TIMES

Supporters of gun rights rallied outside a secure perimeter at the Virginia State Capitol on Monday, in Richmond, Va.

But a gradual demographic shift has emerged in the state — suburbs have boomed, and the ratio of Virginians in rural areas has shrunk. When Democrats flipped the State Legislature in the fall and won control of the state government for the first time in a generation, they pledged, in part, to swiftly seek new limits to guns. All of that has thrust Virginia into a tense battle over gun rights, and into the center of a national cultural divide.

"People feel their values are under attack and the emerging liberal elite are either unaware or unresponsive," Bob Holsworth, a political analyst in Richmond, said of the rally, which the police said drew 22,000 people to the Virginia State Capitol and the wind-chilled streets around it.

For several days, the authorities had been bracing for the possibility of violence, fueled by reports that white supremacists, armed militia groups and other extremists planned to attend the rally, which

VICTOR J. BLUE FOR THE NEW YORK TIMES

Armed demonstrators gathered near the Virginia State Capitol building on Monday to protest gun control.

was organized by the Virginia Citizens Defense League. In the end, the police reported no major incidents or violence and announced only one arrest, of a woman accused of wearing a bandanna to cover her face after being warned not to. (It is illegal in the state to wear a mask in public to conceal one's identity.)

The F.B.I. on Thursday had announced the arrest of several people associated with the Base, a white extremist, anti-government group that aims to establish a white "ethno-state," including three men who had obtained weapons and had discussed attending the rally.

Citing credible "threats of violence," Governor Northam declared a state of emergency before Monday's demonstration and temporarily banned all weapons from the Capitol grounds.

About 6,000 people without weapons made their way into the main protest area after waiting in line to go through metal detectors. Thousands more, some proudly displaying firearms and wearing camouflage clothing, packed nearby streets. There were military-style rifles, shotguns, 9-millimeter handguns, .45- and .22-caliber pistols, and even a .50-caliber sniper rifle.

Chris Dement, 22, said that he was glad to see the demonstration was peaceful but that he was prepared to use a 9-millimeter carbine — which he brought to stand in solidarity — for self-defense in case of violence.

"It's never out of the realm of possibility," he said.

Shannon Watts, the founder of Moms Demand Action, an organization that wants stronger gun laws, wrote on Twitter that "gun extremists" had gathered "in an attempt to intimidate lawmakers out of doing what voters elected them to do: pass common-sense gun laws that will keep our families safe."

Officials hoped to prevent the kind of deadly clash that engulfed a far-right rally in Charlottesville, Va., in 2017, when conflict between white nationalists and counterprotesters ended in the death of a counterprotester and left dozens injured.

Amid fears of a potential conflict, gun control activists delayed a vigil for victims of gun violence until hours after the rally ended. More than a dozen students, including some who had survived school shootings, waited in an office in the General Assembly building throughout the pro-gun rally, listening to shouting and cheers outside.

"Intimidation is not peaceful," said Andrew Goddard, the legislative director for the Virginia Center for Public Safety, who led the group in a moment of silence for the thousands of people who have been killed in shootings.

Some gun rights supporters at the rally said they had always planned to carry out a peaceful demonstration, and felt unfairly associated with violence. Teri Horne, 51, of Quitman, Texas, stayed outside the weapons-free area, carrying her rifle. "This is where freedom began, right here, and this is what they're doing to the people of Virginia," Ms. Horne said as she pointed at police officers screening demonstrators.

ALYSSA SCHUKAR FOR THE NEW YORK TIMES

Hours after the rally, a small group of gun control advocates held a vigil at the State Capitol.

Since Virginia Democrats took control of the Legislature, they have been racing to make a mark on state policy, and gun control has been atop their agenda. Last week, the State Senate approved three gun control bills that the House of Delegates could approve as early as this week. The measures limit purchases of handguns to one each month; require that gun buyers submit to background checks; and allow local governments to ban guns in parks and public buildings. Mr. Northam has said he would sign the bills.

But the fates of other limits, including a proposed ban on assault-style rifles, remain uncertain, and the state is still starkly divided on the issue, complicating political choices. In recent weeks, more than 100 municipalities have designated themselves “sanctuaries” for the Second Amendment. Though the measures are purely symbolic, lawmakers and sheriffs in those areas have said they will refuse to enforce new gun control laws.

ALYSSA SCHUKAR FOR THE NEW YORK TIMES

Dick Heller, known for the U.S. Supreme Court case District of Columbia v. Heller, speaking at the rally on Monday.

President Trump, who lost Virginia in the 2016 election despite winning the rural, less populous parts of the state, has repeatedly drawn attention to Virginia's debate over guns in recent days, warning that state Democrats were threatening Americans' right to bear arms. On Monday, he wrote about the issue on Twitter, urging people to vote Republican. "I will NEVER allow our great Second Amendment to go unprotected," he wrote, "not even a little bit!"

At the rally, support for Mr. Trump was apparent amid the banners and flags and shouts of "U.S.A." A large "Make America Great Again" flag whipped above the crowds that gathered outside the State Capitol perimeter. A bus adorned in pro-Trump posters, including a "Women for Trump" flag and a flag with the president's head photoshopped on Rambo, occasionally drove past the entrance of the Capitol grounds and was greeted with cheers from the crowd.

Dick Heller, the lead plaintiff in a lawsuit that led to a landmark Supreme Court decision in 2008 holding that the Second Amendment protected an individual's right to keep and bear arms, drew roars from the crowd when he read parts of the amendment aloud. The Democrats, he said, "want to make us like Baltimore, Detroit, Venezuela, Chicago!"

Mr. Heller asked the crowd, "Do we need gun control in Virginia?"

The crowd roared back: "Nooooo!"

As the rally went on, occasional chants went up: "No confiscation! No registration!"

Vinny McMahon, 25, drove to the rally from his home in Maryland. "I don't think the governor should be telling anyone what to do," said Mr. McMahon, who brought one of his guns with him. "I want the ability to defend people around me."

TIMOTHY WILLIAMS, **SABRINA TAVERNISE** and **ZOLAN KANNO-YOUNGS** reported from Richmond, and **SARAH MERVOSH** from New York. **NEIL MACFARQUHAR** contributed reporting from New York.

SABRINA TAVERNISE is a national correspondent covering demographics and is the lead writer for The Times on the Census. She started at The Times in 2000, spending her first 10 years as a foreign correspondent.

ZOLAN KANNO-YOUNGS is the homeland security correspondent, based in Washington. He covers immigration, border issues, cybersecurity, transnational crime and other national security threats.

SARAH MERVOSH is a national reporter based in New York, covering a wide variety of news and feature stories across the country.

Glossary

adjudicate Decide by a judge.

appellate court A court that reviews lower courts decisions and hears appeals.

assault-style weapon A semiautomatic firearm with a magazine that detaches, generally for use by the military.

background check A process that inquires into a person's criminal, educational and employment history.

bipolar disorder A mood disorder that includes periods of depression alternating with those of mania.

due process A guarantee of fair, lawful proceedings.

epidemiology A medical branch that deals with detecting the source and cause of infectious diseases.

gun buyback A program designed to purchase firearms owned by the public, generally conducted by the police.

incumbent A person who holds a political office.

infringe To violate a person's rights.

involuntary hold A legal process in which a person is confined in a psychiatric hospital by a court of law.

iterative Repetitious.

litigation An ongoing lawsuit.

national gun registry A listing of all the firearms in the country.

open-carry states States where it is legal to carry a firearm in the open instead of concealed.

partisan Someone who is fiercely devoted to a political party.

red-flag laws Laws which allow the removal of firearms from people who are judged to pose an imminent threat.

Second Amendment The part of the U.S. Constitution that protects an individual's right to keep and bear arms.

semiautomatic firearm A weapon that can discharge bullets one after another.

subpoena A legal demand for a person to appear before a court of law.

Media Literacy Terms

"Media literacy" refers to the ability to access, understand, critically assess and create media. The following terms are important components of media literacy, and they will help you critically engage with the articles in this title.

angle The aspect of a news story that a journalist focuses on and develops.

attribution The method by which a source is identified or by which facts and information are assigned to the person who provided them.

balance Principle of journalism that both perspectives of an argument should be presented in a fair way.

bias A disposition of prejudice in favor of a certain idea, person or perspective.

byline Name of the writer, usually placed between the headline and the story.

commentary A type of story that is an expression of opinion on recent events by a journalist generally known as a commentator.

credibility The quality of being trustworthy and believable, said of a journalistic source.

editorial Article of opinion or interpretation.

feature story Article designed to entertain as well as to inform.

human interest story A type of story that focuses on individuals and how events or issues affect their life, generally offering a sense of relatability to the reader.

impartiality Principle of journalism that a story should not reflect a journalist's bias and should contain balance.

intention The motive or reason behind something, such as the publication of a news story.

interview story A type of story in which the facts are gathered primarily by interviewing another person or persons.

motive The reason behind something, such as the publication of a news story or a source's perspective on an issue.

news story An article or style of expository writing that reports news, generally in a straightforward fashion and without editorial comment.

op-ed An opinion piece that reflects a prominent individual's opinion on a topic of interest.

paraphrase The summary of an individual's words, with attribution, rather than a direct quotation of their exact words.

plagiarism An attempt to pass another person's work as one's own without attribution.

quotation The use of an individual's exact words indicated by the use of quotation marks and proper attribution.

reliability The quality of being dependable and accurate, said of a journalistic source.

rhetorical device Technique in writing intending to persuade the reader or communicate a message from a certain perspective.

source The origin of the information reported in journalism.

style A distinctive use of language in writing or speech; also a news or publishing organization's rules for consistent use of language with regards to spelling, punctuation, typography and capitalization, usually regimented by a house style guide.

tone A manner of expression in writing or speech.

Media Literacy Questions

1. Identify the various sources cited in the article "Tennessee Expands Gun Rights" (on page 12). How does Katharine Q. Seelye attribute information to each of these sources in her article? How effective are Seelye's attributions in helping the reader identify her sources?

2. "Defying N.R.A., Texas Lieutenant Governor Favors Background Checks on Private Gun Sales" (on page 33) and "With Florida Shooting Survivors, N.R.A. Spokeswoman Holds Back. With Conservatives, It's a Different Story." (on page 74) are articles involving the N.R.A. Look for author bias in both pieces. Are you able to detect any? If so, identify possible reasons for this bias.

3. "In a Face-off With the N.R.A., San Francisco Blinks" (on page 48) features a photograph of Wayne LaPierre, the C.E.O. of the N.R.A. What does this photograph add to the article?

4. What is the style and tone of "Nation Reels After Gunman Massacres 20 Children at School in Connecticut" (on page 64)? How does this affect the purpose of the article? Why do you think this is?

5. Does "Adam Lanza's Mental Problems 'Completely Untreated' Before Newtown Shootings, Report Says" (on page 71) use multiple sources? What are the strengths of using multiple sources in a journalistic piece? What are the weaknesses, if any?

6. What is the intention of the article "A Gun Killed My Son. So Why Do I Want to Own One?" (on page 89)? How effectively does it achieve its intended purpose?

7. In "Some With Histories of Mental Illness Petition to Get Their Gun Rights Back" (on page 111) and "In Gun Debate, a Misguided Focus on Mental Illness" (on page 153), both authors cover mental illness and guns. How are the interviews and approaches between authors and their subjects the same? How are they different?

8. Is the article "The Gun Rights Tilt" (on page 150) a compelling example of an op-ed? Identify how Ross Douthat's attitude and tone help convey information about the topic.

9. "Don't Blame Mental Illness for Gun Violence" (on page 156) is an example of an editorial by the New York Times Editorial Board. Why do you think the board issued this editorial? Is the editorial effective?

10. What type of story is "Why Doesn't America Know More About Gun Safety?" (on page 181)? Can you identify another article in this collection that is the same type of story? What elements helped you come to your conclusion?

11. Identify each of the sources in "More Retail Chains Ask Customers Not to Carry Guns Openly" (on page 190) as a primary source or a secondary source. Evaluate the reliability and credibility of each source. How does your evaluation of each source change your perspective on this article?

12. Does Jacey Fortin demonstrate the journalistic principle of impartiality in her article "Beto O'Rourke Urges Banks to Cut Services for Gun Sales" (on page 197)? If so, how did she do so? If not, what could Fortin have included to make her article more impartial?

Citations

All citations in this list are formatted according to the Modern Language Association's (MLA) style guide.

BOOK CITATION

THE NEW YORK TIMES EDITORIAL STAFF. *Gun Rights: Finding the Balance.* New York Times Educational Publishing, 2021.

ONLINE ARTICLE CITATIONS

ASTOR, MAGGIE. "Newtown Wasn't an End for Gun Control. It Was a Beginning." *The New York Times*, 29 Apr. 2019, https://www.nytimes.com/2019/04/29/us/politics/newtown-parkland-guns.html.

BARRON, JAMES. "Gunman Kills 20 Schoolchildren in Connecticut." *The New York Times*, 14 Dec. 2012, https://www.nytimes.com/2012/12/15/nyregion/shooting-reported-at-connecticut-elementary-school.html.

COWAN, ALISON LEIGH. "Adam Lanza's Mental Problems 'Completely Untreated' Before Newtown Shootings, Report Says." *The New York Times*, 21 Nov. 2014, https://www.nytimes.com/2014/11/22/nyregion/before-newtown-shootings-adam-lanzas-mental-problems-completely-untreated-report-says.html.

DOUTHAT, ROSS. "The Gun Rights Tilt." *The New York Times*, 24 July 2012, https://campaignstops.blogs.nytimes.com/2012/07/24/the-gun-rights-tilt/.

EPSTEIN, REID J., AND THOMAS KAPLAN. "On Gun Control, 2020 Democrats Agree: No Reason to Hold Back." *The New York Times*, 12 Aug. 2019, https://www.nytimes.com/2019/08/12/us/politics/2020-democrats-gun-control.html.

FORTIN, JACEY. "Beto O'Rourke Urges Banks to Cut Services for Gun Sales." *The New York Times*, 12 Sept. 2019, https://www.nytimes.com/2019/09/12/us/politics/beto-o-rourke-guns-banks.html.

FRIEDMAN, RICHARD A., M.D. "A Misguided Focus on Mental Illness in Gun

Control Debate." *The New York Times*, 17 Dec. 2012, https://www.nytimes.com/2012/12/18/health/a-misguided-focus-on-mental-illness-in-gun-control-debate.html.

GIBSON, GREGORY. "A Gun Killed My Son. So Why Do I Want to Own One?" *The New York Times*, 1 June 2019, https://www.nytimes.com/2019/06/01/opinion/sunday/shooting-laws-guns.html.

HAKIM, DANNY. "Clashing Senate Reports and New Questions on the N.R.A." *The New York Times*, 27 Sept. 2019, https://www.nytimes.com/2019/09/27/us/nra-senate-reports.html.

HAKIM, DANNY. "In a Face-off With the N.R.A., San Francisco Blinks." *The New York Times*, 1 Oct. 2019, https://www.nytimes.com/2019/10/01/us/san-francisco-nra-faceoff.html.

HUSSEY, KRISTIN, AND ELIZABETH WILLIAMSON. "Supreme Court to Weigh Taking Bellwether Case Against Gun Industry." *The New York Times*, 5 Nov. 2019, https://www.nytimes.com/2019/11/05/us/politics/supreme-court-remington-sandy-hook.html.

KURLANTZICK, JOSHUA. "Global Gun Rights?" *The New York Times*, 17 Sept. 2006, https://www.nytimes.com/2006/09/17/magazine/17wwln_essay.html.

LICHTBLAU, ERIC. "State Focus and Infusion of Funding Buoy Gun Control Advocates." *The New York Times*, 3 Jan. 2016, https://www.nytimes.com/2016/01/04/us/politics/state-focus-and-infusion-of-funding-buoy-gun-control-advocates.html.

LIPTAK, ADAM. "Justices Won't Hear Case on Waiting Period for Gun Purchases." *The New York Times*, 20 Feb. 2018, https://www.nytimes.com/2018/02/20/us/politics/supreme-court-waiting-period-gun-purchases.html.

LIPTAK, ADAM. "Second Amendment Case May Fizzle Out at the Supreme Court." *The New York Times*, 2 Dec. 2019, https://www.nytimes.com/2019/12/02/us/politics/second-amendment-supreme-court.html.

LIPTAK, ADAM. "Supreme Court Still Divided on Guns." *The New York Times*, 2 Mar. 2010, https://www.nytimes.com/2010/03/03/us/03scotus.html.

LIPTAK, ADAM. "Supreme Court Will Review New York City Gun Law." *The New York Times*, 22 Jan. 2019, https://www.nytimes.com/2019/01/22/us/politics/supreme-court-guns-nyc-license.html.

LUO, MICHAEL. "Answers on Felons and Gun Rights." *The New York Times*, 15 Nov. 2011, https://thelede.blogs.nytimes.com/2011/11/15/answers-on-felons-and-gun-rights/.

LUO, MICHAEL. "Felons Finding It Easy to Regain Gun Rights." *The New York Times*, 13 Nov. 2011, https://www.nytimes.com/2011/11/14/us/felons-finding-it-easy-to-regain-gun-rights.html.

LUO, MICHAEL. "Some With Histories of Mental Illness Petition to Get Their Gun Rights Back." *The New York Times*, 2 July 2011, https://www.nytimes.com/2011/07/03/us/03guns.html.

THE NEW YORK TIMES. "Don't Blame Mental Illness for Gun Violence." *The New York Times*, 15 Dec. 2015, https://www.nytimes.com/2015/12/16/opinion/dont-blame-mental-illness-for-gun-violence.html.

THE NEW YORK TIMES. "An Ominous Reversal on Gun Rights." *The New York Times*, 14 May 2002, https://www.nytimes.com/2002/05/14/opinion/an-ominous-reversal-on-gun-rights.html.

THE NEW YORK TIMES. "States' Rights vs. Gun Rights." *The New York Times*, 2 Mar. 2010, https://roomfordebate.blogs.nytimes.com/2010/03/02/states-rights-vs-gun-rights/.

THE NEW YORK TIMES. "Watch Out, America — The Supreme Court Is Back in Session." *The New York Times*, 5 Oct. 2019, https://www.nytimes.com/2019/10/05/opinion/sunday/supreme-court-abortion.html.

THE NEW YORK TIMES. "What Bolstering Gun Rights Will Mean." *The New York Times*, 28 June 2010, https://roomfordebate.blogs.nytimes.com/2010/06/28/what-bolstering-gun-rights-will-mean/.

THE NEW YORK TIMES. "Why Doesn't America Know More About Gun Safety?" *The New York Times*, 7 Aug. 2019, https://www.nytimes.com/2019/08/07/opinion/guns-shootings-research.html.

QIU, LINDA, AND JUSTIN BANK. "Checking Facts and Falsehoods About Gun Violence and Mental Illness After Parkland Shooting." *The New York Times*, 16 Feb. 2018, https://www.nytimes.com/2018/02/16/us/politics/fact-check-parkland-gun-violence-mental-illness.html.

ROJAS, RICK, AND KRISTIN HUSSEY. "How Sandy Hook Families Hope to Pierce the Gun Industry's Legal Shield." *The New York Times*, 8 Apr. 2019, https://www.nytimes.com/2019/04/08/nyregion/sandy-hook-gun-lawsuit.html.

ROSENTHAL, ANDREW. "Out of State Guns." *The New York Times*, 9 Apr. 2012, https://takingnote.blogs.nytimes.com/2012/04/09/out-of-state-guns/.

SEELYE, KATHARINE Q. "Tennessee Gun Bills Poke at Democrats, Washington." *The New York Times*, 15 June 2009, https://www.nytimes.com/2009/06/16/us/16tennessee.html.

Stolberg, Sheryl Gay. "As Trump Weighs Gun Safety Bills, Barr's Plan Draws Skepticism." *The New York Times*, 18 Sept. 2019, https://www.nytimes.com/2019/09/18/us/politics/trump-barr-gun-safety.html.

Stolberg, Sheryl Gay. "Lawmakers Court Trump on Gun Safety, With Some Appealing to His Ego." *The New York Times*, 20 Sept. 2019, https://www.nytimes.com/2019/09/20/us/politics/congress-trump-guns.html.

Stolberg, Sheryl Gay. "Pelosi and Schumer, in Push for Gun Safety Legislation, Urge Trump to Defy N.R.A." *The New York Times*, 9 Sept. 2019, https://www.nytimes.com/2019/09/09/us/politics/schumer-pelosi-trump-gun-control-letter.html.

Streitfeld, David. "With Move to Limit Gun Sales, Facebook Is Caught in Debate." *The New York Times*, 5 Mar. 2014, https://bits.blogs.nytimes.com/2014/03/05/facebook-to-crack-down-on-illegal-gun-sales/.

Victor, Daniel. "With Florida Shooting Survivors, N.R.A. Spokeswoman Holds Back. With Conservatives, It's a Different Story." *The New York Times*, 22 Feb. 2018, https://www.nytimes.com/2018/02/22/business/media/dana-loesch-nra-cpac.html.

Vigdor, Neil. "Defying N.R.A., Texas Lieutenant Governor Favors Background Checks on Private Gun Sales." *The New York Times*, 6 Sept. 2019, https://www.nytimes.com/2019/09/06/us/dan-patrick-texas-nra.html.

Williams, Timothy. "Trump on Virginia Gun Dispute: 2nd Amendment 'Under Very Serious Attack.' " *The New York Times*, 18 Jan. 2020, https://www.nytimes.com/2020/01/18/us/virginia-guns-trump.html.

Williams, Timothy, et al. "Amid Tight Security, Virginia Gun Rally Draws Thousands of Supporters." *The New York Times*, 20 Jan. 2020, https://www.nytimes.com/2020/01/20/us/virginia-gun-rally.html.

Zraick, Karen. "More Retail Chains Ask Customers Not to Carry Guns Openly." *The New York Times*, 6 Sept. 2019, https://www.nytimes.com/2019/09/06/business/open-carry-walmart-cvs-walgreens.html.

Index

This book is current up until the time of printing. For the most up-to-date reporting, visit www.nytimes.com.